TOP 50 JOB-CREATING INDUSTRIES OF THE NEXT DECADE

Stephan S. Sunn

Davidson Global & Co.

CONTENTS

PREFACE

In a time of rapid technological change and economic transformation, perhaps no single question echoes quite as loudly within the minds of young people around the world as the question, "Where will I find my place in tomorrow's workforce?" Standing on decades of experience advising global businesses and professionals in different industries, we wrote this book to provide our perspectives with action plans.

We published research papers and books on business transformation, we have felt the heat of industries that continuously evolved, disappeared, and emerged. Our views are not derived from theoretical projections but from actual experience in working with companies and professionals to successfully work through change.

These 50 industries we explore represent more than job opportunities; they represent pathways to careers and entrepreneurial success. Our analysis is firmly rooted in concrete trends that we have observed while guiding clients through transformational changes.

What makes this book different is the pragmatic tone: rather than abstract forecasting, we share lessons learned from our consulting practice, real-world case studies, and strategies for positioning yourself in growing fields. Whether you are a student planning your career path, a professional considering a career pivot, or an entrepreneur looking for opportunities, we try to offer some valuable insights.

Our approach is optimistic, yet realistic. While recognizing that automation and economic uncertainty create challenges, we underscore the opportunities these changes afford. The future of work isn't something that happens to us—it's something we actively shape through our choices and preparations.

We hope this guide will help you identify and seize opportunities matching best with your skills and aspirations. The road ahead may be bumpy, but with the right knowledge, you can create a brighter future than you could ever imagine.

CHAPTER 1:
INTRODUCTION

We stand at the doorway of a new decade where the transformation in the job market has taken on a dimension very unlike any other experienced by humanity. The intersection of technological changes, demographic transitions, and environmental imperatives pushes the job landscape forward with an unprecedented tempo. The next chapter provides the context for our coverage of those 50 future job-creating industries with a deep look at the forces acting and at what skills will be needed.

Employment Trends Around the Globe

Labor markets are an intricate ecosystem, which is constantly in flux due to a myriad of economic, technological, and social forces acting on it. By 2024, remnants of COVID-19 still lingered around the world and had accelerated many previous trends, and introduced other dynamics in the job market.

Rates now stand at 5.8% but vary considerably across regions. Unemployment has declined at a much faster clip in advanced economies—primarily those in North America and Europe—whose numbers are drawing closer to pre-pandemic totals. Recovery in jobs and economic output has been slow for nearly all the emerging economies—most of Latin America and parts of Asia.

The pandemic has also sharpened inequalities in the labor market. Job losses and reduced hours of work have been particularly concentrated on women, young people, and the low-skilled. In the future, repairing these disparities will be integral in building a more inclusive, resilient labor market.

Forward-looking, some of the decisive trends in employment will be:

1. **Digital Transformation**: In almost all sectors, the usage of digital technologies is on the rise; hence, the nature of jobs is changing with each passing day. While some new job categories come into existence, others become obsolete. From Artificial Intelligence and Machine Learning to Blockchain and the Internet of Things, these technologies are not only changing how we work but also what kind of work we do. For instance, AI development creates the need for an AI ethicist and a machine learning engineer, while automating some jobs in data entry and analysis.

2. **Transition to Green Economy**: The whole world is talking about global warming. Consequently, every sector is advocating for greener initiatives. In the process, "green jobs" are on a highly increasing trajectory in renewable energy, sustainable agriculture, and environmental consultancy. The International Labor Organization estimates that the transition to a green economy could result in 24 million new jobs globally by 2030.

3. **Aging Population**: Most developed nations have the issue of an aging workforce. This trend is not only changing the nature of work but is also creating new opportunities in health care, caregiving, and associated services. In Japan, the caregiving industry will face a shortage of 380,000 workers by 2025.

4. **Globalization 2.0**: If the old globalization was about the movement of goods and capital, the new one is about moving services and talent around the world, courtesy of digital platforms and remote work technologies. This trend is driving a whole new set of possibilities for workers in emerging economies to connect to the global job market and also for companies to access global talent.

5. **Gig Economy Growth**: Growing platform-based employment and freelancing reshape the traditional ways of employing or getting employed, having its pros and cons for employees and employers alike. By 2027, more than half of the U.S. workforce

is forecasted to have done some gig work sometime during their careers.

6. **Automation and Human-AI Collaboration**: While automation will continue to displace some jobs, it is also creating new roles that focus on human-AI collaboration. According to the World Economic Forum, by 2025, for example, both humans and machines will spend equal amounts of time on current work tasks.

Macro Trends

1. **The Fourth Industrial Revolution**: This digital revolution, coming from the fusion of biological, physical, and digital, drives innovation. These blurred boundaries across industries build entirely new fields of work. From printed organs to driverless cars, the fourth industrial revolution is really changing the nature of the skills in the workforce and jobs themselves.

2. **Demographic Changes**: From aging populations in developed countries to the youth bulges of emerging economies, the shift in demography is having a profound impact on the nature of labor markets around the world. Shrinking workforces are driving investments in automation and productivity-enhancing technologies in Europe and East Asia, while leaders in Africa and South Asia work to create enough jobs for their young, growing populations.

3. **Climate Change and Sustainability**: Ongoing pressure to manage climate change stimulates jobs not only in new sustainable industries but also modernizes traditional ones. A shift to the low-carbon economy is going to create jobs not only in renewable energy but also in other areas like green building, sustainable finance, and circular economy design.

4. **Geopolitical Factors**: Trade friction, regional wars, and shifting alliances affect global supply chains and the division of labor between nations. This may be reconfiguring manufacturing and

logistics networks through "near-shoring" or "friend-shoring" and, hence, giving rise to new job clusters in certain regions.

5. **Pandemic Aftermath**: Due to the COVID-19 pandemic, many industries, including job markets, have long-term after-effects. These include new consumer behavior and work patterns. This shift has accelerated the use of e-commerce, telemedicine, and remote work technologies, which result in the creation of new opportunities but put huge pressure on conventional business models.

6. **Knowledge Economy**: As routine tasks continue to be automated, work that requires knowledge will continue to come at an increasing premium. This shift is increasing demand for higher education and specialized skills, and many are beginning to question what the future of work will look like for workers without advanced degrees.

Skills and Mindsets for Tomorrow's Jobs

As work evolves, so, too, will the required competencies and modes of thinking of the workforce. For jobs of the future, technical proficiency will need to be balanced with cognitive flexibility and emotional intelligence. The focus areas are:

1. **Digital Literacy**: Besides basic computer usage, workers will need to understand and interact with advanced technologies such as AI, big data, and automation systems. This doesn't mean all people have to become programmers, but a basic understanding of how those technologies work and what they imply will be quite important in most industries.

2. **Adaptive Thinking**: With an ever-changing work environment, settings and situations will need to be adapted constantly. This would include skills related to critical thinking, solving problems, and the ability to learn new things rather quickly as the need and time arise.

3. **Creativity and Innovation**: The more routine tasks are automated, the higher the level of creativity and innovative thinking required on the part of humans. It does not just refer to artistic creativity but also to the ability to think outside the box in areas relating to business strategy, scientific research, and product design.
4. **Emotional Intelligence**: Skills such as empathy, communication, and collaboration will be in very high demand in an increasingly global, interdependent labor force. As machines assume more of the purely analytical work, uniquely human capabilities such as emotional intelligence will become major differentiators in the labor market.
5. **Data Analysis**: With the increased utilization of complex datasets, interpretation and insight from these are going to be sought after across industries. This includes much more than just pure technical analysis; rather, there is also the ability to communicate data-driven insights to non-technical audiences effectively.
6. **Sustainability Mindset**: Understanding and practicing sustainability will become one of the key competencies in most professions. It involves not only environmental but also social and economic sustainability.
7. **Cross-cultural Competence**: With the increasing globalization of work and job opportunities, the ability to work across cultures will be a growing imperative. This would also mean language skills, cultural awareness, and the capability to handle different work environments.
8. **Entrepreneurial Spirit**: Besides the conventional work arrangement, an entrepreneurial mindset or the power of initiative, problem-solving, and innovation will be greatly prized. This involves skills like strategic thinking, risk assessment, and the ability to identify and capitalize on opportunities.
9. **Cybersecurity Awareness**: As the workplace and life generally become digital, core knowledge for all types of workers is a basic understanding of the principles of cybersecurity.

10. **Ethical Reasoning**: The development of AI and other powerful technologies means that the ability to understand complex ethical issues in most roles is going to be much more significant.

The concept of the "job for life" is well and truly over. Now, not only must people be engaged in lifelong learning, but also be prepared to make multiple career changes throughout their lives. This change necessitates people acquiring new skills, but more importantly, it requires a growth mindset in people—an attitude toward life where change presents an opportunity, not a threat.

These shifting demands, in turn, will mean a parallel evolution of the education system. Today's traditional four-year degree programs will give way to a more flexible, modular approach with the workforce continuously upskilling and reskilling throughout their careers. Micro-credentials, online learning platforms, and corporate training programs will play an increasingly important role in workforce development.

The people, employers, and governments will share responsibility for developing skills. People will have to take more responsibility for learning and development throughout their lives. Employers should invest in training and upskilling programs if they want to have a competitive workforce. At the same time, governments must develop policies and build infrastructure to support lifelong learning and enable workers to move between sectors as jobs change.

Working one's way through these 50 industries that may shape the job market in the next decade requires keeping in mind these general trends and needs of skill acquisition. After all, the future of work is less a destination than it is a journey of movement. Only from understanding the forces at play can individuals and organizations alike set themselves up for success in this brave new world.

In the following chapters, each of these job-creating industries will be explored in depth, considering both specific opportunities and the required skills in detail. From artificial intelligence, renewable energy, healthcare technology, and creative economy, these are the new frontiers of innovation and job growth for this decade. This is a book that, by the end, gives clear details of the future job destinations and how one prepares for them.

CHAPTER 2: THE TECH-DRIVEN FUTURE

Into the next decade, technology remains the most potent engine of job creation and transformation. The chapter zeroes in on three critical domains of technologies - a set that reconfigures the employment landscape. These are Artificial Intelligence and Machine Learning, Robotics and Automation, and Cybersecurity. Each of these branches opens up new job categories while making a marked impact on many already well-entrenched roles across industries.

Artificial Intelligence and Machine Learning

Artificial Intelligence and Machine Learning are no more concepts alien in the context of science fiction, let alone our daily lives and workplaces. They may easily rank as one of the largest job creators in the decade to come.

AI at the Core of the Fourth Industrial Revolution

The era of the Fourth Industrial Revolution was one of a highly marked integration of digital, physical, and biological systems and touted AI as no less than its very core. AI now handles vast volumes of data and patterns, facilitating intelligent decisions in industries as varied as healthcare and finance to manufacturing and retail.

According to estimates, AI alone will add up to 97 million new jobs by the year 2025, a report from the World Economic Forum projects. While this new technology replaces some of the old jobs, because of this new technology, net job creation shall be positive.

Job Creation in AI and ML

1. Data Scientists and Machine Learning Engineers: In the development, evolution, design, and implementation, including the maintenance, of each AI, many professional experts in this field are required. These emerge as highly sought-after professions for developing algorithms, training models, and driving actionable insights from voluminous data.
2. AI Ethics Officers: With AI taking bigger tasks in decision-making, the focus is shifting towards ethics. The officers ensure that as bias, privacy, and transparency raise red flags, the AI systems are developed and deployed responsibly.

3. Algorithm Developers: These professionals design complex rule sets that will govern AI systems. As applications that involve AI are mushrooming, so will the need for algorithm developers to fine-tune the systems in various industries.
4. AI Trainers and Interaction Designers: With AI systems increasingly being used to deal directly with customers, professionals who understand the details involved in training these systems for natural interaction with humans will be in demand.
5. AI-Assisted Healthcare Professionals: In medicine, AI at present endeavors to enhance human medical expert judgment. New job categories comprise AI-assisted diagnosticians and professionals in personalized medicine.

AI's Influence on Non-tech Industries

AI is not only influencing the tech industry but also a variety of other sectors:

1. Healthcare: AI applications drive diagnostic innovation, drug discovery, and personalized treatment plans. New professions emerging include AI health consultants and medical imaging experts.
2. Agriculture: AI helps with precision farming, managing crops and resources with utmost efficiency. New roles associated with agriculture include agricultural data analysts and AI farm management professionals.
3. Legal: AI is changing the manner of legal research and contract analysis. Even as AI automates some paralegal tasks, new jobs are being created in the form of legal data strategist and AI compliance officer.
4. Manufacturing: AI-powered predictive maintenance and quality control are opening up smart factory manager and AI-assisted design engineer positions .

Robotics and Automation

Robotics and automation represent another significant area contributing to job opportunities, despite misconceptions about robots replacing human workers.

Manufacturing, Logistics, and Services Robotics

1. Manufacturing: The employment of Collaborative robots, working with or alongside humans in factories, is continuing to increase. Because of this growth, job openings such as robotics integration specialists and human-robot interaction designers are now open.
2. Logistics: The industry is changing with automated warehouses and delivery systems. This means that new warehouse automation managers or last-mile delivery robot operators are some of the occupation options one may go for.
3. Services: Service-oriented applications are one of the fastest growing fields of robots in customer service, healthcare, and hospitality. Such growth creates demand not only for

robot programmers with knowledge of service-oriented applications but also for specialists in robot-human interactions.

Key Job Growth Areas in Robotics

1. Robotics Engineers: They design, build, and maintain robotic systems. While robotics systems continue to find broader applications across industries, the demand for robotics engineers continues to improve correspondingly.
2. Automation Consultants: They help businesses identify which processes can be automated and integrate the right solutions into operations, serving as a bridge between emerging technology capabilities and business needs.
3. Maintenance Technicians: Increased usage of robotic systems also demands the application of skilled technicians in maintenance and repair works related to these systems.
4. Robot Ethicist and Policy Maker: Along with the increased application of robots in life, there arises a need for professionals who can provide ethical insights into the use of robots and build proper policies and regulations.
5. Human-Robot Interaction Designers: It is the role of these professionals to ensure safe and productive interaction between humans and robots through proper interface and protocol designing.

The International Federation of Robotics estimates that the worldwide stock of robots will reach 11.5 million units by 2025, indicating a highly positive outlook for robotics-related jobs.

Cybersecurity

In this digital world, cybersecurity is one of the most prime focuses. The rise in these cyber threats has caused an emerging trend in the demand for cybersecurity careers across industries.

According to Cybersecurity Ventures, global damages from cybercrime will cost $10.5 trillion annually by 2025. This figure is really staggering and brings into focus how dire the need is for cybersecurity and cybersecurity professionals. COVID-19 accelerated the shift to remote work, thereby further increasing the demand for cybersecurity experts as companies with distributed workforces operating via the cloud have seen their attack surface expand exponentially

Key Jobs in Cybersecurity

1. White Hat Hackers/Pen testers: They find system and network vulnerabilities before malicious hackers can exploit them. As the attackers become more sophisticated, the white hat hackers must proactively strengthen defenses.
2. Cyber Security Analysts: They test networks for security breaches, investigate incidents, implement security, and establish standards within organizations.

3. Risk Assessors: The cybersecurity risk assessors analyze an organization's digital infrastructure to determine potential security risks and come up with proper mitigation strategies.
4. Cloud Security Specialists: Since cloud computing has come up, the demand for the protection of cloud environments has also increased. This is done by them to ensure that data stored and processed on the cloud remains safe from unauthorized access and cyber-attacks.
5. IoT Security Experts: Since it is gaining momentum rapidly, IoT is considered a source of serious vulnerability. IoT security experts keep pace with their job of securing smart devices and networks against all sorts of possible risks.
6. Cybersecurity Trainers: In a world where human errors are often the root of security breaches, trainers who teach employees how to be safe online are increasingly valuable to organizations.
7. Incident Response Managers: They manage incident response teams during a cyber-attack, develop incident response plans, and manage all relevant stakeholders through crisis management.

According to (ISC)², the global cybersecurity workforce needs to grow by 65% to effectively protect organizations' critical assets, translating into millions of job opportunities worldwide.

The Interconnected Core of Tech-Driven Jobs

While we have discussed AI, robotics, and cybersecurity one by one, it should be noted that all these aspects are actually interrelated. AI is finding its increasing usage in robotics and cybersecurity. Robotics technologies must be defended against cyber threats; on the other hand, cybersecurity itself is leveraging AI and ML to detect and respond to threats more effectively.

This interrelationship gives rise to hybrid positions across disciplines, such as:

1. **AI Cybersecurity Analysts**: Specialists in machine learning algorithms to detect and respond to cyber threats in real-time.
2. **Robotics Cybersecurity Specialists**: Professionals who develop security measures to protect robotic systems from potential cyberattacks.
3. **AI Ethics and Security Consultants**: Experts in handling AI ethics and security matters related to misuse or potential cyber-attacks.

Preparing for a Technological Future

With a future centered on AI, robotics, and cybersecurity, one thing is sure: the pace of change will be incredibly fast. Professionals will be able to achieve the best performance in such a technology-saturated environment with the help of their attention to the following:

1. **Continuous Learning**: With rapid technological changes, continuous learning and upskilling are necessities. Professionals can stay current through online courses, boot camps, and certification programs.

2. **Interdisciplinary Skills**: As technologies become increasingly interconnected, professionals with interdisciplinary skills will be highly valued. For example, combining programming skills with domain knowledge in healthcare or finance can be particularly advantageous.

3. **Soft Skills**: While technical skills are important, soft skills in critical thinking, problem-solving, and communication remain fundamental. These human skills complement technological capabilities and are much harder to automate.

4. **Ethics**: As technology becomes pervasive, understanding its ethical implications will be a key skill. Professionals who can address the ethical challenges related to AI, robotics, and data privacy will be in high demand.

5. **Adaptability**: The rapid pace of technological change makes adaptability essential. A growth mindset – being open to change – will be crucial for long-term career success.

The amount of innovation and career building that will continue to occur as we go even further into this tech-driven future is immense. Yes, some of the traditional roles may get displaced, but overall the trends are toward the creation of jobs and exciting new career paths. Professionals will be well-placed to adapt to the dynamic job market of the future by staying updated with these trends and continually updating their skills.

In the following chapter, we turn to how digital transformation is altering industries outside the tech sector and the new sources of jobs this opens throughout the economy.

CHAPTER 3: DIGITAL TRANSFORMATION & SERVICES

The current technological revolution is sweeping over the labor market. If we want to understand just how enormous an effect it is having, we need to step back and take in the whole vista of digital transformation and the rapidly expanding technology services sector. The panorama has three main parts, and each of these is delivering substantial and rising numbers of jobs to our economy.

1. Cloud computing (and Software as a Service),
2. Big data and analytics,
3. Blockchain and cryptocurrency.

Cloud Computing and SaaS

SaaS (Software-as-a-Service) and cloud-based solutions are transforming how businesses operate and creating numerous new job opportunities. These shifts have lured many into the world of cloud computing, which has become an essential part of modern operations. As demand for cloud computing continues to grow, so does the demand for personnel with cloud computing capabilities.

According to the research firm Gartner, the worldwide public cloud services market will grow 17 percent in 2023, translating to an almost $100 billion expansion in severe recession projections for the moment.

Key Advantages of Cloud Computing

- Scalability
- Cost-efficiency

- Flexibility

These qualities are encouraging companies of every size to move their operations to the cloud. The cloud shift isn't just about the relocation of systems; it's about the reconsideration of business processes and applications in a cloud-native world.

The SaaS Revolution

The SaaS model has revolutionized not just the delivery of software but the very business of software. Companies no longer need to invest in a hefty IT apparatus to access powerful, business-transforming applications. For CRM, ERP, and all sorts of other business functions, SaaS solutions are rapidly becoming the rule rather than the exception.

Career Opportunities in Cloud Computing

1. Cloud Architects design an organization's cloud strategy and implement it. According to the U.S. Bureau of Labor Statistics, this group of jobs is supposed to grow by 25% from 2020 until 2030.
2. SaaS Developers: Develop software as a service that should be user-friendly, secure, and scalable.
3. Cloud Migration Consultants: They are supposed to help organizations transition to cloud operations.
4. Cloud Security Experts: Ensuring data and applications are secure in cloud environments.
5. Cloud Data Engineers: They design and manage data infrastructure in cloud environments.

Big Data and Analytics

We currently exist in an age defined by data, with the scale of data generated and held across the globe reaching almost unfathomable proportions.

- The International Data Corporation (IDC) forecasts that the "global data sphere " will grow from 45.41 zettabytes in 2019 to 175 zettabytes by 2025.
- The McKinsey Global Institute (MGI) projects that the volume of data will double at least every four years for the next decade.

Applications of Big Data

"Big Data" has been incorporated in a variety of industries for insight, better decisions, and very personalized customer experiences:

- Finance: Algorithmic trading and fraud detection
- Healthcare: Personalized medicine, improved patient outcomes
- Retail: Personalized marketing, optimization of inventories, price decisions

Career Opportunities in Big Data and Analytics

1. Data Analysts: They process data, do the calculations, and derive insight from the data.
2. Machine Learning Experts: Development of algorithms on complex applications, including recommendation systems.
3. Data Governance Specialists: Formulate and implement policies towards responsible data handling, ensuring follow-through on regulations.
4. Data Engineers: Construct and maintain infrastructures of big data, ensuring efficient collection, storage, and processing.
5. Data Scientists: Analyze and interpret data in relation to business implications. Blockchain and Cryptocurrency

Blockchain and Cryptocurrency

The new digital economy run by blockchain technologies and cryptocurrencies is more than just finance. There are new professions appearing in fintech, DeFi, and blockchain technologies.

The worldwide blockchain market is estimated to grow from $7.18 billion in 2022 to $163.83 billion by 2029—a compound annual growth rate (CAGR) of 56.3% (Fortune Business Insights, 2023).

Applications of Blockchain

Beyond finance, industries from supply chain management to healthcare are exploring blockchain for record-keeping and system integration.

Career Opportunities in Blockchain and Cryptocurrency

1. **Blockchain Developers**: Design and implement blockchain protocols and smart contracts.
2. **Crypto Asset Managers**: Manage crypto portfolios and understand the unique aspects of crypto markets.
3. **Blockchain Legal Experts**: Navigate the legal challenges arising from blockchain technology and cryptocurrencies.

The Interconnected Nature of Digital Transformation

Cloud computing, big data, and blockchain work in concert as common facets of digital transformation:

- Cloud computing serves as the basis for big data.
- Big data acts as a powerful engine for insight and intelligence necessary for digital transformation progress.
- AI and machine learning have improved SaaS applications and their underlying economic models.
- These technologies combine to create cloud-native, big data-capable, and highly secure blockchain SaaS applications.

Career Preparation in Digital Transformation and Technology Services

To prepare for a career in these rapidly changing fields, focus on two key areas:

1. **Lifelong Learning**: Continuously supplement your core knowledge with fresh concepts learned through various digital means (e.g., online courses, webinars).
2. **T-Shaped Skill Set**: Develop a broad understanding across multiple disciplines to gain a comprehensive perspective on the complex ecosystem of digital transformation and technology services.

The industries that will generate the most jobs over the next ten years are mainly digital. The relentless tide of job creation in the tech sector and beyond is being driven by digital transformation. As one industry after another goes digital, the push is on to find a workforce that can manage this digital journey. This is not a narrative without some casualties, though; it comes with a warning that some old jobs may be rendered obsolete.

CHAPTER 4: HEALTH CARE REVOLUTION

An unprecedented opportunity for the transformation of the global healthcare industry exists today. The current revolution in the industry brought on by technological advances, an evolving demographic, and an increasingly expectant patient base offers stunning prospects not only for job creation but also for the innovation of health-related products and services. The surge of opportunity is concentrated in three seemingly frontline areas: biotechnology and personalized medicine; telemedicine and health tech; and the foundational aspect of an aging population and its often-demanding need for geriatric care.

Biotechnology and Personalized Medicine

The intersection of genetic research, biopharmaceuticals, and artificial intelligence will unleash a new prototype in the field of personalized medicine. This field is predicted to offer the applications of medical treatment to a unique individual considering his or her genetic makeup, lifestyle, and environmental considerations.

Growth Drivers

1. Advances in Genomic Sequencing Technologies
2. Cost of Genetic Testing is Falling and available locations get more extensive
3. Big Data and AI in Healthcare: Analyzing Progress and Quantitative Prediction
4. Targeted Therapies on the Rise

Emerging Job Roles

1. **Genetic Counselors**: These are professionals who help the patients understand and make informed decisions about the results of genetic testing. In the midst of increased genetic testing, the need for qualified genetic counselors will go up many folds.
2. **Biotech Researchers**: Scientists specializing in fields like gene therapy, CRISPR technology, and biopharmaceuticals will hold the keys for next-generation treatments.
3. **Personal Health Consultants**: This is a professional group that, at the intersection of medicine, genetics, and lifestyle management, will help the individualist derive a personalized health plan.
4. **Bioinformatics Specialists**: With the spewing of genetic information from different sources on an increase, this field will retain a specific demand for specialists who can analyze and interpret such information.

Global Perspective

Having said this, the personalized medicine market is about to witness phenomenal growth in all regions. North America and Europe will continue to be at the forefront in research and development, but it is the emerging markets of Asia and Latin America that are catching up really fast, with ever-increasing healthcare expenditure coupled with government initiatives.

Telemedicine and Health Tech

The COVID-19 pandemic accelerated the adoption of telemedicine and digital health platforms, changing the fundamentals of the way healthcare would be delivered and managed.

Growth Drivers

1. Increase in wireless penetration and internet connectivity
2. Need for accessible healthcare in remote areas
3. Rising costs of healthcare and efforts toward efficiencies and affordability

4. Advances in IoT and wearable technologies

Emerging Job Roles

1. **Telehealth Consultants**: These are professionals who will assist healthcare providers in implementing and optimizing solutions on telemedicine and integrating these seamlessly into existing systems.
2. **Digital Health System Developers**: Software engineers with experience in healthcare applications will contribute to the creation of user-friendly, secure platforms in telemedicine and health management.
3. **Remote Diagnostics Specialists**: They will merge medical knowledge with technological expertise to design and implement systems that can deliver accurate, remote assessments of patients.
4. **Virtual Reality Therapists**: As VR technology improves, therapists who are specialists in the use of VR for the treatment of PTSD, phobias, and chronic pain will be sought after.

Global Perspective

Although the developed world is driving most of the adoption of telemedicine, growth opportunities abound in emerging markets. Large rural population-based countries like India and China are investing big in telemedicine to bridge the urban-rural divide in health care.

Aging Population and Geriatric Care

The Increase in life expectancy worldwide, coupled with decreasing birth rates in most countries, has increased the demand for specialized care services among the elderly.

Growth Drivers

1. Increased life expectancy in both developed and developing nations
2. Low birth rates leading to an inverted population pyramid

3. Increased Burden of age-related chronic diseases
4. Technological innovations in assistive care

Jobs of the Future

1. **Geriatric Care Specialists**: There will be a greater demand for qualified health professionals as health issues, particularly those concerning older adults, become increasingly complex.
2. **Home Healthcare Aides**: As more seniors would prefer to age in place, competent home health workers will remain in high demand.
3. **Developers of Healthcare Technologies**: Engineers and developers who develop supportive technologies to enable independent living among seniors, including fall detection systems and smart home solutions, will find ample opportunities.
4. **Gerontechnology Consultants**: Such professionals will provide advice on the assessment and recommendation of technologies appropriate for improving the quality of life in old age.

Global Perspective

While Japan leads the way in terms of addressing the many challenges of an aging society, many countries throughout Europe and North America are literally not far behind. Most economies in the emerging world, especially in Asia, have either just begun or will soon begin to experience this demographic transition promising market indeed for innovative geriatric care solutions.

The Road Ahead

Thus, the healthcare revolution creates great opportunities both for job creation and for improving the quality of patient care. Still, there are those that raise problems to be overcome, such as:

1. **Privacy and security in patients' data**: With an increase in digital health, great care has to be taken to keep private data secure.

2. **Regulatory frameworks**: The speed with which innovation occurs often outpaces existing regulatory frameworks; innovative approaches to regulating healthcare must therefore be agile and forward-looking.
3. **Setting the Tone Right**: Societal ethical issues in development around gene editing, AI-driven diagnostics, and so many other areas beg for answers.
4. **Healthcare Equity**: This is about equal access to increasingly personalized, technology-driven care and shall be one of the challenges that will need to be tackled.
5. **Workforce Training**: As healthcare evolves, continuous upskilling and reskilling are necessary to keep pace with technological advancements.

The healthcare revolution has opened an ocean of opportunity for all kinds of professionals. From biotechnology to tailored medicine, from telemedicine to geriatric assistance, the future of health care promises to be more tailored, accessible, and efficient than ever.

These are the emerging trends that are very important in strategic planning and decision-making by executives and policymakers. Thus, investment in the right technologies that drive innovation, coupled with human resource development, positions organizations, and countries at the forefront of this healthcare revolution.

Moving ahead, collaboration between public and private sectors, including cross-border collaborations, would remain at the core in dealing with global health challenges for delivering the full benefits of these revolutionary changes in healthcare delivery and management.

CHAPTER 5: GREEN ECONOMY AND SUSTAINABILITY

When pressing challenges like climate change and environmental degradation, the transition to a green economy has been a global imperative. In fact, this transition is not only an environmental imperative but also one of the biggest drivers of economic growth and employment generation. Sectors contributing to the green economy range in scope from renewable energy and clean technology to sustainable agriculture and practices involving the circular economy. The next chapter presents those sectors of the green economy that are especially promising, based on how much employment they are likely to create over the coming decade.

Renewable Energy and Clean Tech

The renewable energy sector is at the forefront of the revolution in the green economy. In the face of commitments by countries globally to reduce their carbon footprint and move away from dependence on fossil fuels, the level of investments in solar, wind, and other clean sources of energy continues to skyrocket.

Solar Power

The industry has fantastically grown with the advances in its technology and general cost reduction. Professions in this field comprise manufacturing, fitting, installation, and research into better photovoltaic technologies. While the industry at present is pioneered by countries such as China, the US, and

Germany, the emerging markets in Africa and Southeast Asia are putting up a pace in the adoption of solar.

Wind Energy

Onshore and offshore wind farms are growing across the world. Thus, it will need wind turbine technicians, engineers in aerodynamics and material science, and project managers for large-scale installation of wind farms. Countries with longer coastlines like the UK, Denmark, and Japan are keener on investing in offshore wind farms.

Energy Storage

As more and more renewable sources are integrated, the demand for effective solutions in energy storage becomes increasingly crucial. In this subsector, innovation in battery technologies in addition to energy has huge implications for electric vehicles and consumer electronics. Professions related to this field include everything from engineers of batteries to new energy storage materials chemists to grid integration specialists.

Smart Grid Technologies

The integration of renewable energies into the existing power grids involves a number of management systems at the back. Thus, it opens vistas for software developers, systems engineers, and data analysts who are capable of managing and optimizing energy distribution and consumption.

Key Roles:

- Renewable Energy Engineers
- Energy Storage Specialists
- Smart Grid Developers
- Sustainability Consultants

Circular Economy and Waste Management

The concept of the circular economy, where waste is minimized and resources are reused or recycled, is taking off around the world. In contrast to the traditional linear economy model, it creates new jobs and changes many others in various industries.

Waste-to-Energy

These technologies convert waste into usable energy. Presently, these technologies have become very sophisticated. The sector needs engineers who can design and operate the systems and logistics experts who can manage the complex supply chains in collecting and processing the wastes.

Recycling and Upcycling

Advanced recycling technologies make possible the recycling of materials that could not be recycled earlier. There is, therefore, an increasing demand for materials scientists and chemical engineers, along with product designers, who can make products with a view to recycling and upcycling.

Product Life-cycle Management

With increasing awareness, more and more companies are considering product design with considerations for longevity, repairability, and finally recycling. This sets up a slew of job opportunities in product design, supply chain management, and sustainability officers that apply circular economy principles throughout the whole product life cycle.

Sharing Economy Platforms

The online sharing and reuse platforms of products have, in themselves, contributed to the circular economy. This has opened opportunities for software developers, user experience designers, and community managers to build and manage these platforms.

Key Roles:

- Circular Economy Strategists
- Waste Management Engineers
- Sustainable Product Designers
- Sharing Economy Platform Developers

Sustainable Agriculture and Agri-tech

The agricultural sector is under immense pressure to adapt to climate change and, at the same time, find ways to diminish its environmental impacts. Thus, innovation is constantly being driven by more sustainable farming practices and agricultural technologies.

Precision Farming

Deployment of IoT sensors, drones, and data analytics in farms is transforming not only the way crops are grown but also the resources utilized. This opens wide doors for agricultural data analysts, drone operators, and IoT specialists who shall help farmers optimally organize their activities.

Vertical Farming

This has become increasingly feasible in cities as urbanization is going on. The vocation needs experience in hydroponics, aeroponics, and controlled environment agriculture. Jobs entitled in this area consist of vertical farming systems engineers, plant scientists, and managers of urban agriculture.

This includes concerns about the sustainability of agricultural product sourcing and transportation. Because of this, sustainability-focused supply chain managers and carbon footprint analysts who can track and reduce emissions are being created along the entire agricultural supply chain.

Biotech in Agriculture

Biomolecules would be used to create hardier and more sustainable crops. It is also a field that needs geneticists, agronomists, and biotechnology researchers who could create crops better suited to unpredictable climatic changes.

Key Roles:

- Agrotechnology Engineers
- Vertical Farming Engineers
- Sustainable Supply Chain Managers
- Agricultural Biotechnologists

Green Construction and Infrastructure

It is one of the leading emitters, but at the same time, it leads in popularizing sustainable solutions. Green building practices and projects of sustainable infrastructure emerge with all sorts of professions in high demand.

Green Building Design

Architects and engineers with specializations in sustainable building design are highly sought after. This includes expertise in passive solar design, energy-efficient HVAC systems, and the use of sustainable building materials.

Retrofitting of Existing Buildings

With many cities aiming to reduce their carbon footprint, a growing demand is also emerging for professionals who can retrofit buildings in existence to make them more energy-efficient. It opens up opportunities for energy auditors, insulation specialists, and green HVAC technicians.

Green Planning and Sustainable Urban Planning

Both developing and developed cities across the world are looking to sustainability and resilience from the concept of climate change. In effect, this creates jobs for urban planners who are able to design green spaces, come up with transport systems that are eco-friendly, and plan climate adaptation strategies.

Green Infrastructure

The infrastructure of development working in tandem with nature includes bioswales for stormwater management and green roofs. Landscape architects, civil engineers, and ecologists who can design and implement such solutions are in increasing demand.

Key Roles:
- Sustainable Architects and Engineers
- Energy Efficiency Consultants
- Urban Sustainability Planners
- Green Infrastructure Specialists

Transitioning to the green economy not only represents an environmental imperative but also a major driver of employment and economic growth. Opportunities for meaningful and rewarding careers within this sector include renewable energy, circular economy practices, sustainable agriculture, and green construction.

This unique mix of technical know-how and deep knowledge regarding environmental questions will be in very high demand as we move into a more sustainable future. The Green Economy needs workers who not only have the specific technological know-how but are adaptable and can commit to lifelong learning as new solutions emerge.

This means that policymakers, education institutions, and business leaders would need to invest in the development of green skills and facilitate routes for transitioning workers into these new roles. This way, the shift to a green economy can tackle not only our environmental challenges but also provide wide economic opportunities.

The green economy represents a paradigm shift in how humankind thinks about economic development and the use of natural resources in the environment. As the sector continues to grow, it will determine the future of jobs around the world opportunity to answer some of our most pressing environmental questions with support for innovation and economic prosperity.

CHAPTER 6: GLOBAL TRADE AND EMERGING MARKETS

The pace and scale of changes in global trades today are like nothing we have seen before, and they are presenting a host of difficulties and prospects for businesses and professionals in the field. Three main sectors hold great promise for driving new job and career opportunities in global trade and emerging markets:

1. Global e-commerce and logistics
2. Trade and investment promotions (country, city, and tech parks)
3. The global outsourcing and services sector (city, tech park, and service provider)

Global E-commerce and Logistics

Cross-border e-commerce growth has been explosively reshaping the global retail landscape. As more consumers in different countries depend on international online marketplaces for their shopping requirements, businesses are racing to adapt their strategies and infrastructures to cater to this growing demand.

Rise of Cross-Border E-commerce

Cross-border e-commerce is expected to take a huge share of retail sales worldwide during the next decade. Several factors are driving this:

- Enhanced methods for digital payment and currency conversion
- Enhanced logistics networks, allowing faster and more reliable international delivery options

- Enhanced consumer comfort level when purchasing from foreign retailers
- Enhanced use of mobile devices and internet connectivity in emerging markets

Innovation in Logistics

Because cross-border e-commerce is booming, innovation in logistics and supply chain management has been rapid. The focus has been on:

1. Solutions for last-mile delivery: Companies are pouring resources into developing the technologies and strategies that will optimize the delivery of their products in what we call the "last mile." This includes drone delivery, the use of autonomous vehicles, and local pickup points.

2. Automated warehouse systems: Advanced robotics and artificial intelligence (AI) are working together to make the new generation of warehouse systems more efficient and much more accurate when fulfilling orders.

3. Blockchain across the supply chain: An increasing number of companies are using blockchain technology in ways that promise greater security, transparency, and traceability of products throughout the supply chain.

Career Opportunities

In the field of e-commerce and logistics, this development is sure to yield an increasing amount of job opportunities, including:

- E-commerce strategists focused on cross-border trade
- Supply chain technologists with special emphasis on the optimization of cross-border logistics
- Logistics automation specialists, developing and applying the latest technologies

- Data analysts focusing on global consumer behavior and cross-border purchasing trends

Trade and Investment Promotion

The global economic landscape has become so intricate that the role of trade and investment promotion has never been as crucial as it is today. Governments and private sector organizations are rolling up their sleeves to support international trade and attract FDI. Unlike the presumptions of old corporate executives, trade and investment promotion are handled cooperatively by governments and private sectors. The importance of governments' roles is probably more than that of private corporations in developing countries.

Government Initiatives

Many governments are either setting up or expanding their trade promotion agencies to assist domestic businesses in accessing international markets. These agencies generally focus on:

1. Provide local businesses with market intelligence and counsel on exporting.
2. Conduct trade missions and take part in international trade fairs.
3. Match domestic suppliers with buyers from overseas.
4. Represent and promote favorable trade policies and agreements.

Private Sector Support

The private sector is also contributing significantly to trade and investment promotion:

1. **Consultancy firms**: Specialized services to support enterprises in better understanding the complexity of international trade and expansion.
2. **Financial institutions**: Products and value-added services catering to the specific needs of companies engaged in cross-border trade.

3. **Technology Platforms**: Development of e-marketplaces and other digital tools to make it easier for buyers and sellers to connect across borders.

Investment Attraction

Countries are increasingly competing over foreign direct investment. Therefore, more professionals are needed who can successfully promote investment opportunities and help foreign businesses enter the local economy. This involves:

1. Developing and implementing national or regional investment attraction strategies
2. Establishing and managing programs that offer incentives for investments
3. Guiding foreign investors through the local regulatory and business environment

Career Opportunities

Exciting career prospects in trade and investment promotion include:

- Specialized trade advisers in specific industries or regions
- Market entry consultants to help businesses enter new international markets
- Foreign direct investment experts in investment attraction and facilitation
- Digital trade professionals specializing in e-commerce and digital services exports

Global Outsourcing and Services Sector

The outsourcing industry is constantly evolving worldwide due to continuous changes in technology and business needs. While traditional outsourcing hubs like India and the Philippines are still leading players in this sector, new ones are emerging, and the level of sophistication in outsourced services has also matured.

Shifting Global Outsourcing Landscape

Some trends shaping the future of global outsourcing include:

1. **Shift to high-value services**: Increasingly sophisticated work such as data analytics, software development, and R&D are being outsourced.
2. **Nearshoring on the rise**: Firms are increasingly turning to outsourcing to neighboring countries to reduce time zone differences and cultural barriers.
3. **Automation and AI**: While potentially depressing demand for certain types of outsourced labor, these technologies create new opportunities for value-added services.
4. **Focus on cybersecurity**: Data protection is becoming a key concern, leading to significant investments in security by outsourcing providers.

The Gig Economy and Remote Working

The global pandemic accelerated the gig economy's growth, forcing a shift to remote working. This trend blurs the line between employment and outsourcing, offering new opportunities for:

1. Specialist services delivered on a freelance basis to clients worldwide
2. Firms accessing talent from any part of the world without relocation headaches
3. Development of platforms and tools to enable remote work and project management

Emerging Outsourcing Hubs

While established outsourcing destinations remain important, new ones are emerging, including:

1. **Eastern Europe**: With its skilled workforce, especially in technology and software development
2. **Latin America**: Benefiting from proximity to North American markets and a growing tech sector
3. **Africa**: Slowly rising as an outsourcing destination, especially in countries that have improved their infrastructure and education systems

Career Opportunities

The changing global outsourcing and services sector opens various career paths, including:

- Outsourcing strategists developing appropriate outsourcing solutions for companies managing global operations
- Remote work managers with expertise in distributed team management
- Cross-border team leaders with culture-specific communication skills
- Cybersecurity experts handling threats related to outsourcing contracts

The future of global trade and emerging markets offers myriad opportunities for those ready to navigate the complexities it presents. From rapidly expanding cross-border e-commerce to accelerating logistics innovation and changing the nature of global outsourcing, professionals with the required skillset and mindset to approach such challenges confidently will be in high demand.

In this dynamic environment, the development focus should be on:

1. A global mindset and cultural intelligence

2. High degree of digital literacy and familiarity with emerging technologies
3. Flexibility and commitment to ongoing learning and upskilling
4. Regional or sectoral specialization allied with an overview of global economic trends

Embracing these attributes while keeping a finger on the pulse of evolving global trade and emerging markets will place professionals at the cutting edge of new job creation over the next decade.

CHAPTER 7: CREATIVE INDUSTRIES AND DIGITAL CONTENT

The creative industries are being reborn in a big way, thanks to our increasingly digital world and the rapid technological advancements it has brought. Consumer habits are also changing, and they're changing in ways that are benefiting the key sectors of the creative economy—most notably job growth. This chapter spotlights a few of those key sectors—digital media and entertainment, gaming, and influencer marketing—and delves into what kind of work and what kinds of workers will be needed in the next chapter of their histories.

Digital Media and Entertainment

The digital revolution has fundamentally transformed the world of media and entertainment among all the affected industries or sectors. Traditional content creation and distribution methods are being transformed or displaced totally by innovative digital platforms. The fundamental trend offers new opportunities for content creators, technologists, and strategists.

Live-streaming Services and Subscription-based Models

The emergence of a new generation of content delivery platforms such as Netflix, Amazon Prime Video, and Disney+ has altered the cadence of content creation, distribution, and consumption. These change how we view the content of news, entertainment for ever. These streaming giants have triggered a demand explosion for original content, leading to the rise of new positions and the transformation of existing ones:

- **Content Creators**: With streaming platforms investing heavily in original material, there's an increasing need for professionals who can create and manage digital content sustainably. These creators must understand audience preferences by platform and optimize content for digital consumption.
- **Broadcast Streaming Media Advisors**: Businesses and content providers seek individuals experienced in maximizing the reach and impact of streaming services. These consultants guide clients through digital distribution, rights management, and audience engagement processes.
- **UX/UI Designers**: User experience is paramount in this competitive space. Designers who can create intuitive, compelling interfaces for streaming applications and platforms are in high demand.

The Rise of Original Content

On-demand services have evolved from mere content aggregators to major producers of original content. This transformation has led to a boom in various creative industry roles:

1. Scripting and Directing: Opportunities are popping up for creative professionals who can fashion stories that will engage digital audiences with platform-specific content. Scriptwriters and directors, naturally, take on the bulk of this work. But the types of stories being told—and how they're told—have shifted in recent years in ways that are really interesting to look at, especially in the context of platforms like Netflix.
2. Digital Effects: In the writing and directing section above, I mentioned the idea that the streamed content measures up to the production quality found in the theatrical and broadcast worlds. I can say the same thing here for visual effects artists. Whether it's the streaming behemoth Netflix or a smaller subscription service, the production values across the board have increased, which puts visual effects artists in high demand.

3. Strategy: We know streaming services want more subscribers. But they also don't want people leaving once they've signed up. These two factors—that makeup as much of a subscription service's "game" as anything else—are why content strategists at various services matter more than ever.

Monetization and Advertising in Digital Media

The advent of digital media has shaped new ways of advertising and monetization. As platforms experiment with different revenue models, new opportunities emerge:

- **Digital Advertising Specialists**: Professionals who can navigate the complex world of programmatic advertising, native content, and platform-specific ad formats remain highly relevant.
- **Monetization Consultants**: They help content providers and platforms optimize revenue streams by balancing user experience with effective monetization strategies.

Gaming Industry and Interactive Technologies

The gaming industry has grown into an international giant, consistently outpacing other entertainment sectors in terms of revenue and cultural influence. They are expected to be a formal game in future Olympic Games. The convergence of gaming with cutting-edge technologies, especially VR and AR, opens up new horizons for innovative opportunities and job prospects.

E-sports Development

The growth of competitive gaming has transformed video games into a spectator sport, developing communities of professional players, teams, and leagues. This emerging sector has given rise to several specialist roles:

- **E-sports Event Organizers**: Professionals who can organize large-scale gaming tournaments and handle logistics as well as broadcast aspects of such events.
- **Team Managers**: Responsible for managing professional gaming teams, from business and strategy to hiring/fitting players, negotiating sponsorships, and ensuring performance management.
- **E-sports Content Producers**: Producing engaging content around gaming competitions, such as live streams, highlight reels, and behind-the-scenes features.

Augmented and Virtual Reality in Gaming

As immersive technologies mature, they are reconfiguring the game experience and requiring a range of new skills:

- **Hardware - VR/AR Developers**: Professionals who can build experiences that seamlessly blend the digital and physical worlds in ways that even designers couldn't have imagined.
- **Software - Experience Designers**: Tasked with creating immersive, interactive environments that extend far beyond the conventional limits of game development.

Cross-Platform Gaming and Cloud Gaming

With the movement toward cloud-based game platforms and cross-platform gaming, new technical and strategic positions are emerging:

- **Cloud Gaming Infrastructure Experts**: Professionals who can design and maintain complex backend systems needed to enable seamless cloud gaming.
- **Cross-Platform Development Professionals**: Developers who can create consistent experiences across a wide array of devices and platforms.

Influencers and Social Media Platforms

The influencer economy has emerged as a powerful force in digital marketing and sales, creating new paths for content creators and marketers. Their impact on society and public opinion has increased tremendously last several years. No one can ignore the "Hot Internet Figures" now.

Influencer Marketing

As brands increasingly partner with influencers to reach target audiences, the industry has fostered focused roles such as:

- **Influencer Marketing Managers**: Expected to find, hire, and manage multiple relationships between brands and social media influencers to meet marketing goals.
- **Content Monetization Experts**: Individuals who teach influential ways to monetize their digital presence through sponsorships, affiliate marketing, and branded content.

The Creator Economy

The growth in content creation and access platforms has brought about new supportive roles, including:

- **Digital Brand Consultants**: Professionals providing advice on personal branding, content strategy, and audience engagement to create long-term careers for influencers in the digital space.
- **Community Managers**: Engaged individuals who help creators and their communities of admirers forge relationships to build online communities.

The Role of Algorithms

Understanding and leveraging the power of algorithms is crucial for driving success in the digital content space. This involves:

- **Algorithm Specialists**: Professionals who deconstruct and interpret social media algorithms to help content developers and brands maximize reach and engagement.

- **SEO Optimization for Social Media**: Specialists who apply SEO principles to social media content, ensuring all content is optimized for maximum discoverability through the platform's search functionality.

Digital transformation is happening all around us, but it seems to be particularly powerful in the creative industries. Here, writers, producers, and artists are engaged in figuring out how to work with the new technologies at their disposal. And, smart or not, their choices will foretell our next chapter: how we will interact with technology, how we will consume media, and how we will express ourselves in the digital age.

These industries have always been about illumination, and whether through the brilliant or dark choices of visionaries, that's where the future will take us—whether it's to an exceptionally compelling virtual reality, as some insist; a digitally gamified day-to-day existence, as others argue; or some other yet-to-be-conceived environment, powered by artificial intelligence.

CHAPTER 8: EDUCATION & KNOWLEDGE -ECONOMY

The education sector is undergoing dramatic transformations, driven by two powerful forces—the rapid development of new technology and the changing demands of the workforce. The U.S. Department of Education has begun to spotlight "lifelong learning" as a guiding force in the shift to an "education for all" model. With more and more opportunities and innovations unfolding in the knowledge economy, this chapter focuses on some of the key trends in the education sector and the spectrum of job opportunities that arise from them.

E-learning and EdTech

Digital learning platforms have radically changed access to education from literally anywhere in the world. Insubstantial players like Coursera, edX, and Udacity democratized learning by creating MOOCs, Massive Open Online Courses, which disrupted the traditional model of education. Such platforms are actually designed to deliver flexibility and accessibility; one could gain new skills or knowledge inside the four walls of their bedroom or at a pace that best suits them.

EdTech innovations are remodeling the way one learns:

1. Gamification makes learning interactive and fun; hence, engagement and retention increase.

2. Virtual and Augmented reality created an immersion in learning that was previously constrained to medicine and engineering.
3. Adaptive learning technologies make education personalized for students by automatically regulating the difficulty of content based on each student's performance.

Careers in EdTech also continue to emerge:

- EdTech Developers design and develop intuitive and effective digital learning platforms.
- Instructional Designers develop engaging online course content and curricula.
- Learning Analytics Specialists use data to improve learning outcomes and personalize learning.

Corporate Training and Lifelong Learning

In the face of rapid technological change, skills development has become an urgent imperative. Large Companies Put on Educator Hat: Companies are up-skilling and re-skilling their workforce at a rate never seen before as labor markets tighten and firms try to stay ahead. Micro-credentials and digital badges allow professionals to demonstrate specific competencies and knowledge gained through focused learning experiences.

Innovative approaches characterizing corporate learning include:

- Hybrid learning models whereby online and offline training together leads to total effectiveness.
- Just-in-time learning and performance support tools allow the employees to search for information at the point of need.

- Social learning platforms for knowledge sharing.

In corporal learning, job roles are emerging and constantly evolving:

- Learning and Development Specialists design training programs that promote organizational objectives.
- Corporate Trainers conduct effective learning in an engaging and constructive manner on various platforms.
- Design Learning Experience Designers develop corporate training for maximum retention and application.

STEM and Digital Skills Development

With the increasing importance of science, technology, engineering, and mathematics to development and economic growth, the failure to address the worldwide STEM skills gap has remained a troublesome headache for governments and industries everywhere. Running parallel to this trend has been the starting-to-take-flight ideas for increasing diversity and inclusion in STEM, thus potentially tapping into a wider talent pool.

Digital integration into curricula is key:

- Coding and computational thinking are becoming part of K-12 to better prepare the next generation.
- Data literacy and analytics skills become basic knowledge across diverse professions.
- Education in digital citizenship and online safety provides responsible and ethical use of technology.

The popular careers regarding the modern meaning of STEM education include:

- STEM Curriculum Developers: They create interactive and hands-on learning experiences for the next generation of innovators.
- AI and Data Science Educators prepare students for a future driven by data, where advanced concepts in machine learning and data analysis will surface.
- The Educational Technology Integrator helps schools effectively adopt and implement new technologies within the classroom for engaging learning.

Higher Education in the Future

From the changing workforce demands to evolving definitions of what a student is, universities everywhere are re-imagining what it means to pursue a higher education. As such, blended learning models that combine online and on-campus experiences in one education are here to stay. These models provide flexibility for students without sacrificing the advantages of in-person interaction. Competency-based education challenges the status quo of traditional degree programs, focusing on demonstrable skills rather than time spent in the classroom.

Emerging higher education technologies include:

- Blockchains for secure, verifiable academic credentials easily shared and verified by employers.
- AI-powered Academic Advising Systems: to help students navigate their complex degree requirements and career pathways.
- Virtual Campuses and Global Collaboration Platforms: Connecting students and faculty around the world.

Higher education innovation is opening more ways to careers in the following:

- Education Futurists: forecasters of trends, guide institutional strategy in response to changed educational landscapes.
- Alternative Credentialing Professionals create innovative models of recognition for all the skills and knowledge acquired through various forms of learning experience.
- Academic Industry Liaison Officers correlate and engage the business community at universities to ensure the relevance of the curriculum that then leads to employment.

Riding the Future of Learning

With the education and knowledge economy still evolving, professionals in this line have to adopt continuous learning and adaptability. The dynamic crossroads of technology, pedagogy, and workforce need in constant evolution raise opportunities that are both exciting and impactful. Tuning into these trends and building a diverse skill set could position one well in the dynamic world of education and lifelong learning.

It will be more personalized, available, and totally soaked in technology. As the boundaries continue to blur between formal education, professional development, and lifelong learning, there will be emerging new models of knowledge acquisition and building skills. Those having the vision and capability to help others find their way through the changing landscape- whether as educators, technologists, or lifelong learners-will be uniquely positioned to thrive in the knowledge economy of tomorrow.

In these times of rapid change, education can no longer be confined to traditional institutions and life stages. Education is now a lifelong process indispensable for personal growth and professional success. Moving forward, the ability to learn, unlearn, and relearn will be the most prized skill in an increasingly complex, interconnected world.

CHAPTER 9: MOBILITY AND SMART CITIES

The transformation of the appearance and the operation of transportation and urban living is coming from the intersection of high technology, environmental concerns, and urbanization. Enabled by the Internet of Things and other high technologies, our emerging smart cities offer potential solutions to a range of urban problems—from traffic jams to smog to ineffective resource management. These two new chapters in the urban narrative—one focused on the tech-enabled city and one on the eco-effective city—promise huge job generation and economic growth in the sectors of mobility and smart city development.

Electric Vehicles (EV) and Green Transportation

The shift to electric vehicles is one of the most transformational changes ever seen on roads. With environmental concerns and superior battery technology, the market base for EVs is experiencing exponential growth on a global scale.

Market Dynamics and Government Initiatives

Governments all over the world are offering an array of incentives and are formulating regulations meant to drive worldwide adoption of electric vehicles (EVs). The targets these governments have set for themselves are ambitious and, in some cases, quite astonishing. By 2030, for instance, the European Union intends to have 30 million zero-emission vehicles (mostly

EVs) on its roads. Meanwhile, the United States, as part of a split overall target of having half of all new vehicles be "zero emission" by 2030 and half again by 2035, has set actual road-target sales numbers: 25% by 2030 and 50% by 2035.

Creation of Jobs in the EV Ecosystem

The EV revolution is presenting extremely diversified job opportunities:

1. EV Engineers: Electric powertrain design, battery management systems, and vehicle electrification experts.
2. Battery Technologists: Lithium-ion and next-generation solid-state batteries developers and optimizers.
3. Charging Infrastructure Developers: EV charging network designers and deployers.
4. Supply Chain Managers: Experts who provide services in sourcing and managing sustainable materials for the production of EVs.
5. Recycling Specialists: Individuals engaged in devising efficient ways of reusing batteries.

As the EV market grows and matures, tens of thousands of new jobs will be created both directly and indirectly through manufacturing, research, and ancillary services to replace jobs lost in the more conventional automobile sector. The jobs along the EV supply chain will also be generated when the industry grows to be a pillar of the local market.

Autonomous Vehicles and Self-Driving Technology

Autonomous vehicles are starting to reshape the future of transport by making transport systems even safer, more efficient, and more accessible.

Levels of Autonomy and Market Projections

The Society of Automotive Engineers - SAE - categorizes six levels of vehicle autonomy from Level 0, no automation, to full automation in Level 5. However, the latest, Level 5, full autonomy, is still in the development stages, while partially autonomous features are already widespread in contemporary vehicles.

Market projections are high:

- The global autonomous vehicle market will reach $ 556.67 billion by 2026, at a CAGR of 39.47% during the forecast period, 2019-2026. Allied Market Research
- Adoption of Level 4 and 5 autonomous vehicles is likely to be widely adopted in several developed markets by 2030.

Upcoming Career Opportunities

The industry is generating multiple highly skilled employment opportunities in most of the streams as identified below:

1. Autonomous Systems Engineers: Developers of self-driving algorithms and sensor fusion technologies are called autonomous systems engineers.
2. AI and Machine Learning Experts: Professionals who develop decision-making systems for AVs.
3. Robotics Engineers: Professionals who integrate hardware and software components in AVs.
4. Cybersecurity Experts: Professionals who ensure connected and, importantly, autonomous vehicles are secure.
5. Ethics and Policy Advisors: Those professionals who address ethical and regulatory challenges in deploying AVs.

As the deployments of AVs increase, new roles peculiar to fleet management, specialized maintenance, and AV-specific urban planning will emerge.

Smart Cities and Urban Mobility

Smart cities use technologies to make city living better, and the most important focus area is mobility. Integrations such as IoT, AI, and big data are enabling cities to manage traffic flow more profoundly by reducing emissions and making public transport options even more efficient.

Some Key Technologies in Smart City Mobility

1. Intelligent Traffic Management Systems: Based on AI, this system changes real-time traffic light timing to provide an optimized traffic flow.
2. Smart Parking Solutions: IoT-enabled systems guiding drivers to available parking spaces, reducing congestion and emissions.
3. Integrated Mobility Platforms: Apps integrating a variety of transportation modes-public transit, bike-sharing, and ride-hailing-operated seamlessly for urban mobility.
4. Connected Infrastructure: Smart streetlights, roads, and buildings communicate to vehicles and pedestrians for safety and efficiency.

Career Avenues in Smart City Development

The development of smart cities opens vistas in a plethora of career directions in the following ways:

- Urban Data Scientists: The specialists who can analyze information about cities to inform policy and infrastructure decisions.
- IoT Solution Architects: Experts in designing and implementing connected device networks in urban environments.
- Sustainable Urban Planners: Those experts take into consideration green technologies and smart mobility solutions in the design of cities.
- Smart City Project Managers: Managers responsible for multi-stakeholder, complex implementations for smart cities.
- MaaS - Mobility-as-a-Service Strategists: Experts who can integrate public-private transport options into single, integrated

transportation solutions.

As cities around the world continue to invest in smart technologies, these positions will play a significant role in defining what living spaces in urban areas will continue to look and feel like in the future.

The Future of Urban Air Mobility

Urban Air Mobility -UAM represents the next frontier that transportation systems are undertaking in the development of smart city environments. This is enabled through eVTOLs, which have the potential to change the way people move within urban areas.

Market Potential and Technological Advancements

The global UAM market is expected to reach a value of USD 15.2 billion by 2030, growing at a CAGR of 11.33% from 2025 to 2030. Some of the key developments to watch are:

- Advances in electric propulsion and advanced batteries to make air travel efficient and "green."
- Advances in autonomous flight systems to ensure safety and operational cost reduction.
- Development of vertiports and air traffic management systems to integrate UAM into urban environments.

Upcoming Career Profiles in the UAM

The UAM industry is creating strange job opportunities, such as the following:

1. EVTOL Aircraft Designers: Those who have successfully designed electric flying vehicles.
2. UAM Infrastructure Planners: These are specialists who can develop and integrate vertiports into city environments.
3. Air Traffic Management Specialists: Experts in systems to manage low-altitude urban air traffic.

4. UAM Safety and Regulatory Experts: Experts in understanding the regulatory environment for urban air mobility.

With the maturing of UAM technology, manufacturing, operations, and supporting services will create a substantial number of jobs.

Charting a Course for Mobility's Future

The prospects opening in front of smart cities and the future of mobility embark on a never-before-seen journey of innovation, sustainability, and economic opportunities. As such, these industries will continue to open up a wide range of high-skilled jobs, including engineering, data science, urban planning, and policy development.

How Professionals Can Capitalize on This Opportunity:
1. The development of the student's interdisciplinary competencies to combine technical experience with an understanding of urban dynamics and principles of sustainability.
2. Keeping pace with the rapid change in technologies and regulatory landscapes regarding mobility and smart city development.
3. Worldwide outlook: cities in all parts of the world adopt and adapt smart mobility solutions.
4. Continuous learning will be necessary because technological development and changing urban needs will require continuous learning.

As we progress in the perspective of moving towards electric, autonomous, and connected mobility within smart urban environments, the potential for transformational changes becomes unparalleled. Those who master the challenge of constant evolution will shape the future of the cities, therefore making them more sustainable, efficient, and livable for future generations.

CHAPTER 10: FINTECH AND FINANCIAL INNOVATION

The financial services industry is at the cusp of a revolution of momentous proportions enabled by technological innovation. This revolution, better known as the FinTech revolution, is fast changing the way people and businesses access, manage, and use financial services. In this chapter, we cover some of the key trends in FinTech and financial innovation, the new types of jobs that have emerged, and how best to get the necessary skills to be employable in this fast-changing sector.

The FinTech Revolution

FinTech is a broad category of innovations that are changing the face of traditional financial services. From mobile banking to digital payment systems, robo-advisors, and blockchain technology, FinTech has come a long way in making financial services more accessible and efficient for users.

Global FinTech Scenario

FinTech markets around the world are growing at a galloping pace:

- There are predictions that the global FinTech market, which was valued at $111.2 billion in 2019, will reach $698.48 billion by 2030 while growing at a CAGR of 20.3% - Research and Markets.
- In 2021, investment in FinTech companies reached $91.5 billion globally, with the U.S., U.K., and India leading in funding,

according to KPMG.
- China and Southeast Asia have become the latest hotspots for FinTech, propelled by high smartphone penetration and underserved populations.

Key Segments in FinTech

1. Digital Banking and Neo Banks
2. Digital Payments and Mobile Wallet
3. Peer-to-Peer Lending
4. Robo-Advisors and WealthTech (Weather Tech)
5. InsurTech (Insurance Tech)
6. Blockchain and Cryptocurrencies

Digital Banking and Neo Banks

Digital banks/neo banks disrupt the traditional concepts of banking to rebuild smooth and mobile-first banking experiences. These banks use technology to minimize operations costs while offering innovative services to customers.

Market Dynamics

- The global neobanking market size is expected to reach $722.60 billion by 2028 and will grow at a CAGR of 47.7% from 2021 to 2028 (Grand View Research).
- Leading neobanks like Revolut, N26, and Nubank are expanding internationally with user-friendly interfaces and low-cost services attracting millions of customers.

Job Roles in Digital Banking

1. **FinTech Product Managers**: They head the development and launching of innovative banking products and features.

2. **UX/UI Designers**: Professionals who create user-friendly and eye-catching digital banking interfaces.
3. **Data Scientists**: Specialists utilize information about customers for personalization of banking services and risk assessment.
4. **Compliance Officers**: Professionals ensure that a digital bank fully adheres to the regulatory requirements, which are usually changing in different jurisdictions.

Digital Payments and Mobile Wallets

The world is going very fast to make the mode of transactions cashless, as people find it very easy to use digital payments and mobile wallets.

Market Trends

- The digital payments market size is projected to grow from $79.3 billion in 2020 to $154.1 billion by 2025, at a CAGR of 14.2% (MarketsandMarkets).
- Mobile wallet adoption is the strongest in emerging markets, mainly led by China through platforms like Alipay and WeChat Pay.

Emerging Roles in Digital Payments

1. **Payment Systems Architects**: Engineers designing secure and scalable payment infrastructures.
2. **Fraud Detection Experts**: Specialists using AI and machine learning to detect and prevent fraudulent transactions.
3. **Cross-border Payment Strategists**: Specialists working to enhance the international payments systems to reduce the cost and speed up processes.

Blockchain and Cryptocurrencies

Blockchain technology and cryptocurrencies offer the potential for changes in financial services, along with further enhanced transparency, security, and efficiency.

Market Developments

- The global blockchain market size is expected to grow from USD 3.0 billion in 2020 to USD 39.7 billion by 2025, at a Compound Annual Growth Rate (CAGR) of 67.3% during the forecast period (MarketsandMarkets).
- All major banks and other central banks are debating studying blockchain use cases, including Central Bank Digital Currencies.

Blockchain and Crypto Jobs

1. **Blockchain Developers**: Engineering that designs and builds decentralized financial applications and smart contracts.
2. **Cryptocurrency Traders and Analysts**: Crypto portfolio managers and market analysts.
3. **Tokenization Experts**: Specialists in the creation and management of digital representatives of real-world assets on blockchain networks.
4. **Regulatory Compliance Managers**: Those who help make sense of shifting regulations regarding cryptocurrencies and blockchain applications.

Artificial Intelligence and Machine Learning in Finance

AI and machine learning are disrupting financial services, from improving customer service to more effective risk management and better investment strategies.

Key Applications

1. **Algorithmic Trading**: AI-driven systems performing trading activities with sophisticated market analysis.
2. **Credit Scoring**: Machine learning models assessing creditworthiness using alternative data sources.
3. **Personalized Financial Advice**: AI-driven robo-advisors providing tailored investment recommendations.
4. **Fraud Detection**: Advanced algorithms identifying suspicious patterns in real-time.

Emerging Roles in AI Finance

1. **AI Financial Analysts**: Specialists developing and implementing AI models for financial forecasting and risk assessment.
2. **Quantitative Traders**: Professionals designing and optimizing algorithmic trading strategies.
3. **AI Ethics Officers**: Experts ensuring the responsible use of AI in financial decision-making processes.

InsurTech: Transforming the Insurance Industry

InsurTech is revolutionizing the insurance sector through innovative products, improved underwriting processes, and enhanced customer experiences.

Market Trends

- The global InsurTech market is projected to reach $158 billion by 2025, growing at a CAGR of 32.7% from 2020 to 2025 (MarketsandMarkets).
- Usage-based insurance and on-demand coverage are gaining traction, enabled by IoT devices and mobile technology.

Job Opportunities in InsurTech

1. **IoT Insurance Experts**: Solution developers of insurance solutions combined with IoT data integrated into the risk assessment models.
2. **Parametric Insurance Innovators**: Experts developing new insurance solutions that would automatically distribute funds dependent on specific pre-defined parameters.
3. **Claims Automation Engineers**: Technocrats designing AI-enabled systems to facilitate faster and smoother claims processing.

Regulatory Technology (RegTech) and Compliance

With the rise in the complexity of financial services along with the high-interconnected global span, RegTech solutions come up for efficient travel through regulatory requirements.

Market Dynamics

- The global RegTech market size will grow from USD 6.3 billion in 2020 to USD 16.0 billion by 2025, at a CAGR of 20.3% (MarketsandMarkets).
- Focus areas also include anti-money laundering (AML) and know your customer (KYC), as well as regulatory reporting.

New Roles in RegTech

1. **RegTech Solution Architects**: Experts in engineering solutions that automate compliance activities.
2. **Regulatory AI Specialists**: Developers of AI technologies that interpret and apply complex regulations.
3. **Cybersecurity Compliance Managers**: Experts who ensure that financial institutions adhere to dynamic cybersecurity rules.

Navigating the Future of Finance

The FinTech revolution has opened up unparalleled avenues for innovation and growth in financial services. As the boundaries continue to blur with the rise of new technologies, professionals will need to be open to continuous learning and changing with the landscape.

Key things to consider when navigating an ever-changing FinTech future:

1. Solid grounding in finance and technology, particularly emerging areas such as artificial intelligence, blockchain, and data analytics.
2. Monitor regulatory updates and the impact of those updates on FinTech innovation.
3. Have a global perspective as FinTech solutions are increasingly borderless.
4. Embrace interdisciplinary collaborations because many FinTech innovations have roots that lie in intersections of finance, technology, and others.

As we move towards a more interconnected and technologically advanced financial ecosystem, those who can navigate this complex landscape will play a crucial role in shaping the future of finance. The potential for transformative change is immense, offering opportunities to create more inclusive, efficient, and innovative financial services that can drive economic growth and improve lives globally.

CHAPTER 11: RETAIL AND CONSUMER GOODS

Radical change is afoot in the retail and consumer goods sectors. This transformation is being propelled primarily by technology—both technological innovation and technological ubiquity—as well as by the influence of an increasingly tech-savvy consumer. Yet, change is also afoot in terms of the...well...change-savvy consumer, who seems, in recent days, to have an almost insatiable appetite for something new or different to be offered unto them. And, you guessed it, always "wowed" by a sustainable offering.

E-commerce Evolution and Omnichannel Retail

The rapid rise in e-commerce, driven by the COVID-19 pandemic, is rewriting retail topographies across the globe. But the victory of e-commerce alone is not the future of retail; it is in seamless online-offline integration and the technological endeavors that make these changes possible at their best.

Global E-commerce Trends

- In 2024, global e-commerce sales are expected to attain $6.3 trillion from $3.3 trillion in 2019 (according to Statista), a fully 100% increase in just five years.
- The percentage of m-commerce contributing to all e-commerce sales will be 72.9% by 2021. The rate will go up with cheaper mobile devices and consumer bases in developing countries.

Omnichannel Strategies

Top retailers implement sophisticated omnichannel strategies, preferably all-in-one offerings.

1. BOPIS Online and pick up in store Convenient for customers Drives traffic to physical stores
2. Ship-from-Store Online orders directly from a store, both in terms of effective management of inventories and delivery
3. Endless Aisle -In the case of offline customers, the items are not available that can be ordered and delivered to them immediately

New Jobs in E-commerce and Omnichannel Retail

1. Operations Managers The online shopper's end-to-end experience, starting with the functionality at the website, through order fulfillment.
2. Omnichannel Strategy Directors will develop and implement integrated retail methods across every customer touchpoint.
3. Digital Merchandising Specialists create curated online product assortments that create engaging digital shopping experiences.
4. Customer Experience Architects will design seamless customer journeys across digital and physical channels.

AI and Data Analytics in Retail

Artificial Intelligence and sophisticated data analytics are revolutionizing retail by enhancing customer understanding, optimizing operations, and informing strategic decisions.

Key Applications

1. **Personalization**: AI-powered recommendation systems offer personalized product suggestions based on individual preferences and behaviors.
2. **Demand Forecasting**: Machine learning models predict consumer demand to optimize inventory levels and reduce waste.
3. **Dynamic Pricing**: AI algorithms adjust prices in real-time based on factors such as competitor pricing and demand fluctuations.
4. **Visual Search**: AI-powered image recognition enables customers to search for products using photos.

Retail AI and Analytics Jobs

1. **Retail Data Scientists**: Analyze large data sets for actionable insights in merchandising, marketing, and operations.
2. **AI Solutions Architects**: Design and implement AI systems for various retail applications.
3. **Customer Insights Managers**: Utilize AI and analytics to develop a deep understanding of customer behaviors and preferences.
4. **Predictive Analytics Specialists**: Develop models to forecast trends, optimize pricing, and enhance supply chain efficiency.

Sustainable and Ethical Retailing

Consumers increasingly base purchasing decisions on retailers' sustainable and ethical practices, compelling the industry to adopt greener and more socially responsible policies.

Key Trends

1. Circular Economy Initiatives: Take-back, refurbishment, and recycling schemes
2. Sustainable Supply Chains: Ethical sourcing, fair labor practice, and carbon footprint reduction
3. Environmental Packaging: Recyclable, biodegradable, or reusable material usage.
4. Supply Chain Transparency and Traceability: It involves the provision of complete information on the origin and production process of the product to the consumer.

New Emerging Roles for Sustainable Retail

1. **Sustainability Director**: Company-wide leaders implementing sustainability programs aligned with core business objectives.
2. **Circular Economy Strategist**: Analysts developing new business models that minimize waste and optimize resource utilization.
3. **Ethical Sourcing Manager**: Ensuring sourced products conform to predefined ethical standards.
4. **Sustainable Product Designers**: Creating products with minimal environmental impact, focusing on recyclability and longevity.

D2C and Brand Ecosystems

The rapid proliferation of D2C brands is disrupting traditional retail models as brands forge closer relationships with consumers and create integrated product ecosystems.

D2C Market Dynamics

- Global DTC market projected to reach $21.25 billion by 2027, growing at a CAGR of 19.2% from 2020-2027.
- Fastest-growing D2C brands such as Warby Parker, Glossier, and Allbirds are rapidly expanding their physical retail footprint on the back of a digital-first approach.

Development of Brand Ecosystems

Major brands are creating comprehensive ecosystems of interrelated products and services:

1. Apple: Ecosystem - Hardware + software
2. Amazon: Ecosystem - Connected devices and services
3. Nike: Digital fitness platforms and product-offering integration

Jobs in D2C and Brand Ecosystems

1. **D2C Brand Managers**: Lead P&L and manage resources to drive brand development and customer acquisition for D2C businesses.
2. **Customer Retention Specialists**: Focus on relationship-building through personal engagement with customers.
3. **Ecosystem Product Managers**: Formulate and manage products and services integrated within brand ecosystems.
4. **Community Engagement Directors**: Build and nurture brand communities to foster customer loyalty and advocacy.

Augmented Reality and Virtual Reality in Retail

AR and VR are transforming retail by bridging the gap between digital and physical spaces.

Key Applications

1. **Virtual Try-Ons**: Allow customers to visualize products like clothes or makeup on themselves.
2. **Immersive Shopping Experiences**: Offer virtual stores or showrooms where customers can explore products in real-time 3D environments.
3. **AR-Enhanced In-Store Navigation**: Provide customers with AR application-based personal in-store guidance and product information.

Emerging Roles in AR/VR Retail

1. **AR/VR Experience Designers**: Create immersive and user-friendly augmented and virtual reality shopping experiences.
2. **3D Asset Managers**: Commission and manage 3D product models for AR/VR applications.
3. **Virtual Store Managers**: Operate virtual retail environments for maximum engagement and sales conversion.

Last-Mile Innovation and Fulfillment

Growing e-commerce demand is driving innovation in last-mile delivery and fulfillment processes.

Main Trends

1. Micro to Small-fulfillment centers: These small-scale, often automated facilities are located nearer to end customers than

conventional warehouses and provide a basis for faster delivery.

2. Robotic delivery: Drones, driverless cars, and other forms of delivery robots promise to provide at least half of all last-mile delivery services.

3. Crowdsourced delivery: Delivery services reliant on large numbers of people doing a little bit for the whole—using apps to guide them—have already hit the big leagues of the multi-billion-dollar convenience sector.

4. Smart lockers: Secure kiosks for package pick-up, strategically located in a surprising number of places, are becoming a convenient and reliable alternative to home delivery.

Last-Mile Innovation Jobs

1. Last-Mile Logistics Managers: Delivery networks that are as rapid as they are efficient are the managers' primary concern.
2. Autonomous Vehicle Integration Specialists: Ensuring delivery vehicle autonomy requires more than meets the eye.
3. Urban Logistics Planners: In contrast to suburban or rural areas, urban deployment introduces far more variables. We plan for them.
4. Fulfillment Technology Directors: The Warehouse is the place where automated fulfillment systems come to life.

Future Perspectives:

Forerunners in the adoption of cutting-edge technologies and in the adjustment to shifting consumer dynamics, the retail and consumer goods sectors have always been among the first to change when new technologies come along. To keep pace with the dynamism of these two industries, their professionals must engage in continuous learning and practice the adaptability that ties technology, consumer experience, and sustainability together.

Here are a few important dimensions along which learning and adaptability will play key roles in the retail and consumer goods industries of tomorrow:

1. Develop profound knowledge of digital technologies and their retail applications, such as artificial intelligence, analytics, and automation—but also AR/VR—which have the potential to revolutionize retailing but have so far been underused.
2. Ensure customers are always top of business operations, and create a seamless, tailored experience in a personalized and memorable way across all channels, including in-store, mobile, and online.
3. Sustainability is becoming a business imperative for business nowadays. Even if you're not selling organic cotton T-shirts, adopting eco-friendly practices can give you a competitive edge. Stay ahead of the game by keeping on top of the latest sustainability-related industry trends and regulations.
4. Establish a clear retail strategy, but also ensure operational agility, so you can pivot as quickly as possible if any of the current headwinds (inflation, interest rates, etc.) shift.

This tech-driven environment, with its nearly indistinguishable physical and digital retail sectors, will reward those who can steer it with heavy influences on the retail and consumer goods industries. It harbors the awesome potential for innovation that will offer opportunities galore to create a more efficient and personalized retail landscape, one that hinges mostly on our evolving demands as consumers and, even more significantly, one that could foreshadow a sustainable world with far less energy- and resource-gobbling retail sector.

CHAPTER 12: THE DARK HORSE INDUSTRIES - UNEXPECTED JOB CREATORS

In this age of talking about established sectors and emerging technologies as primary drivers of job creation, a series of "dark horse" industries are quietly emerging as key sources of employment. Often at the crossroads of technology, sustainability, and changing societal needs, these unexpected job creators are set to play an important role in shaping the future job market.

The following chapter explores three such industries: Vertical Farming and Urban Agriculture, Synthetic Biology and Bio-fabrication, and Digital Ethics and Tech Philosophy. Each of these sectors represents a novel blend of innovation and societal impact, offering professionals from across disciplines a diversified range of opportunities.

Vertical Farming and Urban Agriculture

In line with the increasing urbanization of populations across the globe, coupled with threatening traditional agriculture because of changes in climate conditions, vertical farming, and urban agriculture have emerged as new ways to address food security concerns.

Market Dynamics

- The global vertical farming market is anticipated to reach a value of $21.15 billion in 2028, showcasing a CAGR of 25.7% during the forecast period from 2021 to 2028.
- Some investments by technology companies and venture capitalists will also spur growth in this industry.

Technological Innovations

1. **Hydroponics and Aeroponics**: Soilless cultivation techniques that make the most of space and conserve water at the same time.
2. **LED Lighting**: Specialized lighting system units with utmost efficiency, offering ideal development for plants indoors.
3. **IoT and AI Integration**: Smart sensors and AI algorithms enable monitoring and make real-time adjustments to the growing conditions.
4. **Robotics and Automation**: Systems that automatically plant, harvest, and manage large vertical farms.

Jobs in Vertical Farming

1. **Vertical Farming Engineers**: Experts in designing and optimizing vertical farming systems; they integrate a wide range of technologies to optimize overall efficiency.
2. **Urban Agriculture Managers**: Experts responsible for large-scale urban farming projects; they manage agricultural as well as business operations.
3. **AgTech (Agriculture Tech) Data Scientists**: Experts who analyze data from IoT sensors to optimize yields and resources.
4. **Sustainable Supply Chain Managers**: Professionals who strive to make supply chains efficient and low in carbon for the urban-produced crop.
5. **Vertical Farm Architects**: Specialists who design vertical farms to fit into urban landscapes and buildings.

Impact on Conventional Agriculture

As vertical farming scaling up increases, conventional agriculture will also benefit from new opportunities in the following ways:

- **Precision Agriculture Specialists**: Providing expertise with the application of technologies from vertical farming for improving conventional farming.
- **Agricultural Robotics Engineers**: Those providing design and automated systems applied to both vertical and traditional farms.

Synthetic Biology and Bio-fabrication

Synthetic biology is the redesign of biological systems for useful purposes, an emerging technology with the potential to transform everything from health care to material science in whole new ways.

Market Potential

Global synthetic biology market to reach $30.7 billion in 2026 from $9.5 billion in 2021, at a CAGR of 23.9%. Major applications include pharmaceuticals, sustainable materials, and novel food products.

Key Innovation Areas

1. **Clean Meat**: Manufacturing meat products with cell cultures taken from animals; is more eco-friendly than raising livestock.
2. **Bio-fabricated Materials**: Manufacturing sustainable alternatives to traditional plastics, leather, and other materials through the use of designed organisms.
3. **Custom organisms**: Microorganisms are designed for use in specific industrial processes, such as waste treatment or bio-fuel production.

4. **Synthetic DNA**: DNA-based data storage systems; new uses are foreseen in bio-computing.

Careers Emerging out of Synthetic Biology

1. **Synthetic Biologists**: Professional persons designing biological systems and engineering them for applications.
2. **Bioinformatics Specialists**: These are specialists in using computational tools to analyze and model data of biological relevance.
3. **Biofabrication Engineers**: Such engineers will scale up the production of synthetic biology products from the laboratory to full industrial-scale production.
4. **Bioethics Consultants**: Consultants help organizations work through the ethical implications of applying synthetic biology.
5. **Biomaterials Designers**: Experts designing and creating new materials with unique properties by using systems of engineered biology.

Cross-Industry Impact

Synthetic biology is creating opportunities across a range of sectors:

- **Pharmaceutical Industry**: Specialists in biosynthesis develop and create new ways to manufacture drugs.
- **Fashion Industry**: Bio-textile engineers that create sustainable, biodegradable fabrics.
- **Food Industry**: Cellular agriculture experts that develop lab-grown meat and dairy alternatives.

Digital Ethics and Tech Philosophy

Considering the fact that technology has become embedded within all aspects of society, it could be argued that at no other time in history has there been a greater need for ethical frameworks and philosophical guidance.

Increasingly significant

- The global AI ethics market is projected to attain a value of US$9.1 billion by 2026, while expanding at a 40% CAGR during the forecast period, which ranges from 2021 to 2026. - Xmple Market Research
- Large technology companies, in order to deal with issues concerning the role of their technologies on society, have already started setting up ethics boards and hiring philosophers.

Area of Focus

1. **Ethics in AI**: To overcome bias, ensure transparency, and make AI systems more accountable.
2. **Data Privacy**: lay down guidelines on ethical collection of data, usage, and protection.
3. **Algorithmic Fairness**: How automated decision-making systems can be made non-discriminatory and really fair.
4. **Tech Addiction and Digital Wellbeing**: Psychological impacts of pervasive technology use.
5. **Environmental Ethics of Technology**: Ecological footprint of digital technologies, from data centers onwards.

Emerging Career Opportunities

1. **AI Ethicists**: Those professionals ensure that AI systems are developed and used responsibly, considering the potential impacts on society.
2. **Digital Ethics Consultants**: Those who consult on how companies should address ethical challenges in product development and data usage.

3. **Technology Policy Analysts**: Experts to bridge technological developments with the existing and future regulatory environment.
4. **Digital Well-being Specialists**: Professionals to develop strategies that promote healthy use of technology in personal and professional life
5. **Ethical UX Designers**: Designers responsible for user interface development respectful of user autonomy, contributing to Digital Well-being.

Intersectoral Impact

Need for Digital Ethics Competence:

- **Healthcare**: Bioethicists, in various disciplines involving the use of AI in diagnosis and treatment.
- **Finance**: Ethical AI engineers who implement fairness into algorithmic lending and investment decisions.
- **Education**: Digital ethics educators who develop curricula on the responsible use and development of technologies.

Upcoming Opportunities

These dark horse industries represent the leading edge in innovation and progress that is happening within societies today. Each industry has different opportunities to make an impact. To capitalize on these emerging fields:

1. **Develop Interdisciplinary Skills**: Success often involves a mix of technical expertise, ethical reasoning, and business acumen.
2. **Keep Abreast of Emerging Trends**: Take time to study the latest research and happenings in these rapidly changing fields.
3. **Embrace Continuous Learning**: Along with growth in the industries, new specialization areas are being evolved. In simple words, be ready for adaptability in your career path.
4. **Bearing in Mind Ethical Considerations**: In all of these fields, the demand is emerging for specialists able to deal with

complicated ethical judgments.
5. **Consider Global Perspectives**: All of these industries are in development around the world, and often regions have different approaches. A global outlook will be a necessity.

These dark horse industries represent some of the most important thinking for the future of work and indeed challenging traditional sectoral boundaries. These are more than new vocations; they offer the possibility to tackle some of humanity's most intractable issues: food security, sustainable materials, and ethical deployment of transformative technologies.

In the process, professionals will be one step ahead of the wave of innovations by being able to identify and get ready for such emergent job creators that bring positive change, at the same time building rewarding careers in those fields.

CHAPTER 13: PREPARING FOR THE FUTURE JOB MARKET

As discussed throughout several junctures of this book, the global job market is in the midst of a sea change. It is technological changes and imperatives of sustainability, along with the changing needs of society that are remaking industries and creating new opportunities. This concluding chapter synthesizes the main messages from our exploration of the job-creating industries of the future and develops a strategic framework to enable professionals to successfully navigate an evolving world of work.

Key Trends Shaping the Future of Work

Before entering the strategies of preparation, it is fundamental to remember in brief what the key trends that are going to define the world of jobs in the next decade look like:

1. The nature of jobs in every sector would continue to be changed by technology-driven disruption. New emerging technologies, other than AI and automation, would bring their share of changes too.
2. Sustainability Focus: Transition toward a green economy will ensure that renewable energy, circular economy, and sustainable practices mean newer job creation in these sectors.
3. Digital Transformation: Continued digitization of industries will make digital literacy necessary at all levels of work.

4. Globalization and Remote Work: Better connectivity will ensure increased cross-border collaboration and a chance to work remotely.
5. Aging Population: Demographic shifts will open up new demands in health care, eldercare, and associated services.
6. Lifelong Learning: The rapid pace of change will require continuous upskilling and reskilling throughout careers.

Strategies for Success in the Future Job Market

Adaptability and Continuous Learning

Probably the most important skill for the dynamic job market is being agile. Professionals should cultivate a growth mindset, aiming to commit themselves to lifelong learning.

Key Activities:

- Design and enact a personal learning plan with which you can dedicate time and resources to upskilling on a regular basis.
- Utilize online learning platforms including Coursera or edX, to access leading-edge coursework and micro-credentials.
- Volunteer for stretch assignments and cross-functional projects in your own organization to expand the value of your skill set.

Create a Mix of Technical and Human Skills

While it's true that technology is advancing at an incredible rate, technical skills are still very relevant, but with increasing automation, skills unique to humans are in very high demand.

- Technical Skills: Data analysis, coding, digital literacy, industry-specific technologies.
- Human Skills: Critical thinking, creativity, emotional intelligence, adaptability, complex problem-solving.

Action List:

- Conduct a personal skills audit highlighting areas for personal development.
- Mentoring and coaching on leadership and interpersonal skills.
- Participate in projects that require technical skills, as well as soft skills, for a rounded set of abilities.

Global Mindset

Businesses have become interlinked, and global outlook is crucial to career growth.

Strategies:

- Pursue international assignments or cross-border projects within your organization.
- Take up a second or third language to enhance your ability to work with people from other cultures
- Keep your eyes on the global economic trends, and geopolitical movements that might affect your business.

Data Literacy and Fluency

Across industries, the ability to master digital tools and be able to look at data will be fundamental.

Skills to be Acquired:

- Fluency in basic coding and data analysis
- Knowledge of AI and Machine Learning apps
- Skills in digital collaboration tools
- Data visualization and telling stories of data

What to Do:

- Online courses- acquiring the basics of data science and digital tool studies
- Demonstrate interest in projects that require analytical work on data or any other digitization process.
- Watch for new technologies that will soon be available and may be relevant to your field.

Demonstrate Entrepreneurial Mindset

Entrepreneurial characteristics will be highly coveted, even in the most traditional companies and organizations of employment.

Skills to Acquire:

- Self-motivation and initiative
- Risk evaluation and risk management
- Creativity in problem-solving
- Finding and capitalizing on opportunities

Putting it into Practice:

- Apply intrapreneurship through ideas and leading innovative ventures within your workplace.
- Establish a parallel business or freelance, depending on possible circumstances, in order to test entrepreneurship.

- Join hackathons or innovation challenges to improve your skills in developing and pitching new ideas.

Focus on Sustainability and Ethics

With sustainability soon becoming a new core area of focus in almost all sectors, the more you learn about and implement sustainability, the better.

Action Plan:

- Get certified in management with sustainability or circular economy principles.
- Submit your ideas for sustainability projects in your job or organization today.
- Stay abreast of green regulations and their impact on your sector.

Develop a High-Value Professional Network

A globalized world means having far greater connectivity; which results in great advantages in terms of networking and sharing knowledge opportunities for the workplace.

Ways to Network:

- Involve yourself with professional organizations and industry groups.
- Utilize social media, such as LinkedIn, to leverage connections with leaders in your profession.
- Attend conferences and webinars to stay current on what is happening in your field and to increase your contacts.

Cross-Cultural Competency

With the increasing diversity of today's workplaces and their growing interconnectedness worldwide, the ability to work effectively across cultures has become invaluable.

Opportunities for Development:

- Experience diverse team experiences in your organization
- Participate in cultural exchange programs or international volunteering
- Read about different styles of communicating and ways of doing business across cultures

The Role of Organizations in Preparing for the Future of Work

Whereas individual preparation is important, organizations also play a very significant role in preparing the workforce for the future.

Recommendations for Organizations:

1. Invest in the training of staff to upskill and reskill.
2. Encourage learning and innovation through employees
3. Flexible work arrangements attract the best talent in business.
4. Create diversity, equity, and inclusion in both hiring and promotion.
5. Excellent partnerships with educational institutions in terms of curriculum adaptation in conformity with the present needs of the industry.
6. Investment in the development of human capital while on technology adoption.

Riding into the Future with Confidence

The future job market ensues with challenges and unprecedented opportunities. We must therefore keep ourselves fit to work by being adaptable, continuously learning, and acquiring a diversified skill set.

Some key takeaways could be:

1. Adaptability and lifelong learning are the non-negotiables in the future job market.
2. A blend of technical proficiency combined with strong human skills will be highly valued.
3. Knowledge of digital literacy and a critical ability to read data are factors that will be required in every industry.
4. The global mindset and cross-cultural competencies provide a great environment in which one lives.
5. Entrepreneurial thinking and focus on sustainability are going to drive career innovations forward.

The future of work shall not be something to be reached but rather something that keeps moving forward. With these principles and strategies in place, professionals can confidently walk into the changing landscape and use challenges as opportunities for their growth and impact.

As we wrap up this tour of industries and skills that are going to mark the next decade of work, remember that it is the professionals who adopt a mindset where change is not feared but embraced exciting opportunity to learn, grow, and make their dent in the universe.

CHAPTER 14: 50 INDUSTRIES WITH THE MOST JOB GROWTH

1. Artificial Intelligence (AI)

AI is the backbone of many innovations in sectors like healthcare, finance, retail, and manufacturing. AI technologies such as **machine learning**, **computer vision**, and **natural language processing (NLP)** are reshaping the workforce by automating tasks and making data-driven decisions.

- **Crucial Positions**: AI engineers (build AI systems), machine learning specialists, data scientists (develop models and analyze data), AI ethicists (ensure responsible use of AI), and algorithm developers.

2. Machine Learning

Machine learning (ML) is a subset of AI that enables machines to improve their performance based on data without being explicitly programmed. ML is crucial in applications like **predictive analytics**, **recommendation systems**, and **autonomous vehicles**.

- **Crucial Positions**: ML researchers (create new ML models), AI/ML trainers, predictive modelers (use ML for trend prediction in finance, healthcare, and marketing).

3. Cybersecurity

As cyberattacks grow more sophisticated, **cybersecurity** remains a critical industry. Protecting sensitive data in sectors like **finance**, **healthcare**, and **government** is essential for operational security.

- **Crucial Positions**: Ethical hackers (find system vulnerabilities), cybersecurity analysts, risk assessors, security architects (design secure systems), incident response coordinators (handle breaches).

4. Robotics

Robotics is transforming industries like **manufacturing**, **healthcare**, and **logistics**. Robots perform tasks more efficiently and accurately, from assembling products to conducting surgeries.

- **Crucial Positions**: Robotics engineers (design robots), robotic system integrators (integrate robotics in industries), maintenance technicians (repair and optimize robots), healthcare robotics experts.

5. Cloud Computing

As organizations migrate their operations to the cloud, **cloud computing** services like **Infrastructure-as-a-Service (IaaS)**, **Platform-as-a-Service (PaaS)**, and **Software-as-a-Service (SaaS)** are becoming crucial.

- **Crucial Positions**: Cloud architects (design cloud infrastructure), cloud developers (build apps for cloud environments), DevOps engineers (automate software development and IT operations), cloud migration specialists.

6. Big Data and Analytics

The ability to collect and analyze vast datasets, known as **big data**, is key to understanding market trends, customer behavior, and operational efficiency across industries.

- **Crucial Positions**: Data scientists (analyze complex datasets), business intelligence analysts (use data to inform business strategy), data engineers (build systems to manage large-scale data), data governance officers (ensure compliance with data regulations).

7. Blockchain and Cryptocurrency

Blockchain ensures secure, transparent transactions across multiple sectors, from **finance** to **supply chain management**. The rise of **cryptocurrencies** like Bitcoin and Ethereum is transforming global financial systems.

- **Crucial Positions**: Blockchain developers (create blockchain protocols), smart contract auditors (review code to ensure security), crypto traders (buy/sell digital currencies), decentralized finance (DeFi) experts.

8. Biotechnology

Biotechnology involves using living organisms or biological systems to develop new products in **medicine**, **agriculture**, and **environmental management**. Innovations like gene editing and biopharmaceuticals are at the forefront.

- **Crucial Positions**: Biotech researchers (develop biological solutions), genetic counselors (guide patients on genetic testing), pharmaceutical engineers (develop drugs), bioinformatics specialists (analyze biological data).

9. Telemedicine

Telemedicine uses technology to deliver healthcare remotely, providing patients with access to medical professionals through **digital platforms**.

- **Crucial Positions**: Telehealth specialists (set up virtual care systems), digital health app developers (build platforms for telemedicine), remote diagnostics specialists (interpret remote medical tests).

10. Personalized Medicine

Personalized medicine tailors treatments to individuals based on their genetic profiles, leveraging genomics, AI, and biomarker data to offer customized healthcare solutions.

- **Crucial Positions**: Genetic counselors (advise patients on genetic disorders), personalized healthcare advisors (help design patient-specific treatments), bioinformaticians (analyze patient genetic data).

11. Aging Population Services

The world's aging population is creating demand for specialized **geriatric healthcare** and assistive technologies to improve the quality of life for elderly individuals.

- **Crucial Positions**: Geriatric healthcare workers (provide medical care to older adults), home care aides (assist elderly in daily living), aging tech developers (create tech for seniors like smart homes and wearable health monitors).

12. Renewable Energy

Renewable energy is essential for transitioning to a sustainable, low-carbon economy. **Solar, wind, geothermal**, and **hydropower** technologies are scaling rapidly.

- **Crucial Positions**: Renewable energy engineers (design clean energy systems), solar panel installers, wind turbine technicians, sustainability consultants (optimize energy use).

13. Energy Storage

Efficient **energy storage** systems, especially **battery technology**, are key to managing renewable energy production and ensuring reliable energy supply.

- **Crucial Positions**: Energy storage engineers, battery researchers (develop next-gen batteries), grid infrastructure specialists (manage energy distribution).

14. Circular Economy

The **circular economy** promotes resource efficiency by designing products that can be reused, recycled, or repurposed, aiming to minimize waste and extend product life cycles.

- **Crucial Positions**: Circular economy strategists, recycling engineers, sustainability managers, materials scientists (develop eco-friendly materials).

15. Sustainable Agriculture

Sustainable agriculture uses practices like **precision farming, organic farming**, and **vertical farming** to improve food security while minimizing environmental impact.

- **Crucial Positions**: Agritech engineers (develop farming tech), sustainable farming advisors, precision agriculture engineers (use tech to optimize crop production).

16. Smart Cities

Smart cities use technologies such as **IoT, AI,** and **big data** to optimize urban infrastructure, from traffic management to public services, improving the quality of urban life.

- **Crucial Positions**: Smart city planners (integrate tech into city development), IoT architects (deploy IoT networks in cities), urban sustainability officers (ensure green infrastructure).

17. Electric Vehicles (EV)

The transition from gas-powered to **electric vehicles** is revolutionizing transportation, with growing demand for **charging infrastructure, battery technology,** and **sustainable vehicle design**.

- **Crucial Positions**: EV engineers, battery recycling specialists, charging station technicians, urban mobility consultants.

18. Autonomous Vehicles

Autonomous vehicles (AVs), or self-driving cars, are set to transform transportation, reducing accidents and improving traffic flow while creating roles in AI, sensor technology, and regulatory compliance.

- **Crucial Positions**: Autonomous vehicle engineers, safety testers, AI developers, sensor developers (build the technology that powers AVs).

19. Global E-commerce

With **cross-border e-commerce** expanding, businesses must navigate logistical, regulatory, and marketing challenges in global online sales.

- **Crucial Positions**: E-commerce strategists, supply chain analysts (manage global trade), logistics automation engineers (streamline distribution).

20. Omnichannel Retail

Omnichannel retail creates seamless experiences by integrating online and offline shopping. This allows consumers to browse online, pick up in-store, and return items through various channels.

- **Crucial Positions**: Retail experience managers (ensure a cohesive customer journey), omnichannel strategists, UX/UI designers (design retail apps/websites).

21. Direct-to-Consumer (DTC)

Direct-to-consumer brands bypass traditional retail channels, selling directly through their websites and social platforms.

- **Crucial Positions**: DTC strategists (develop direct sales models), digital brand managers (handle online marketing), customer experience specialists (ensure smooth user interactions).

22. FinTech

The **FinTech** industry uses technology to improve financial services, offering innovations in digital payments, peer-to-peer lending, and online banking.

- **Crucial Positions**: FinTech developers, digital banking analysts (analyze customer behavior in digital banking), blockchain auditors (review blockchain code for security).

23. InsurTech

InsurTech automates and personalizes insurance services using AI and big data, transforming risk assessment and claims processing.

- **Crucial Positions**: InsurTech developers (build digital insurance platforms), claims automation experts (streamline the claims process), insurance product designers (develop personalized insurance policies).

24. WealthTech

WealthTech is transforming wealth management with AI-driven financial advisory platforms, offering personalized portfolio management through robo-advisors.

- **Crucial Positions**: WealthTech developers (build robo-advisors), digital wealth advisors, robo-advisory consultants.

25. EdTech

EdTech is revolutionizing education by offering digital learning platforms, remote teaching tools, and online courses that reach global audiences.

- **Crucial Positions**: EdTech developers, instructional designers (create online courses), digital content creators.

26. Corporate Training

Corporate training programs are increasingly focused on **upskilling** employees in areas like digital literacy, cybersecurity, and data analytics to meet industry demands.

- **Crucial Positions**: Learning and development specialists, corporate trainers, digital content developers.

27. STEM Education

STEM education emphasizes **science, technology, engineering, and mathematics**, essential for building the future workforce.

- **Crucial Positions**: STEM educators, curriculum developers, coding instructors (teach programming skills).

28. Gaming and Interactive Media

The **gaming industry** is booming, driven by advancements in **e-sports**, **virtual reality (VR)**, **augmented reality (AR)**, and **interactive storytelling**. Games are not just for entertainment anymore; they are also used for education, training, and simulations in various fields.

- **Crucial Positions**: Game developers (create the games themselves), VR/AR developers (design immersive gaming experiences), e-sports event managers (organize gaming tournaments), gaming content creators (stream gameplay or create gaming-related media).

29. Digital Media

The shift to **streaming platforms** (like Netflix, YouTube, and Spotify), social media, and online content creation has changed the landscape of **digital media**. Content is now consumed on-demand, creating opportunities in **content production**, **digital advertising**, and **streaming technology**.

- **Crucial Positions**: Digital content creators (create content for platforms like YouTube and TikTok), streaming media consultants (manage and optimize streaming services), digital ad strategists (develop advertising strategies for digital platforms).

30. Augmented Reality (AR)

Augmented reality (AR) enhances the physical world by overlaying digital information through devices like smartphones, glasses, or headsets. AR is being integrated into **retail**, **education**, **real estate**, and **healthcare**, among other industries, transforming customer experiences and learning environments.

- **Crucial Positions**: AR developers (build AR applications), experience designers (design immersive AR environments), AR hardware engineers (develop devices that deliver AR experiences).

31. Virtual Reality (VR)

Virtual reality (VR) creates fully immersive, digital environments and is being adopted in sectors such as **entertainment**, **education**, **military training**, and **healthcare simulations**. VR allows users to interact with these virtual worlds in ways never before possible.

- **Crucial Positions**: VR content developers (create immersive content), simulation engineers (develop virtual training environments for industries like aviation or surgery), experience testers (test and improve VR experiences).

32. Space Exploration

Private companies like **SpaceX**, **Blue Origin**, and **Virgin Galactic** are commercializing **space travel**, while governments continue to invest in space missions for exploration and scientific research. Space technologies also drive innovations in **satellites**, **communications**, and **resource management** in outer space.

- **Crucial Positions**: Aerospace engineers (design spacecraft and technologies), satellite specialists (work on satellite deployment and maintenance), space mining engineers (develop technologies for extracting resources from celestial bodies).

33. Satellite Technology

Satellites play a crucial role in **communication**, **weather forecasting**, **global positioning systems (GPS)**, and **Earth observation**. As satellite technology becomes more accessible and cost-effective, new applications are emerging in **remote sensing**, **agriculture**, and **global internet provision**.

- **Crucial Positions**: Satellite engineers (design and launch satellites), communication experts (optimize satellite-based communications), Earth observation analysts (analyze data for climate change, agriculture, and security purposes).

34. Agritech

Agricultural technology (AgriTech) is focused on increasing the efficiency and sustainability of farming. Innovations include **drones for crop monitoring**, **automated tractors**, **smart irrigation systems**, and **data-driven precision farming**.

- **Crucial Positions**: Agritech engineers (develop farming technology), precision farming consultants (help farmers implement smart technologies), drone operators (use drones for monitoring crop health and yields).

35. FoodTech

Food technology is addressing the global challenge of food production by developing new techniques such as **lab-grown meat**, **alternative proteins**, and **sustainable packaging**. FoodTech also integrates advanced supply chains and automation for food distribution and logistics.

- **Crucial Positions**: Food scientists (research new food sources like plant-based proteins), sustainable product developers (create eco-friendly food products), food supply chain managers (optimize food production and distribution logistics).

36. Waste Management

As the world prioritizes **sustainability, waste management** has become a critical industry focused on recycling, waste-to-energy processes, and reducing landfill use. Innovations such as **smart recycling, composting technologies**, and **biodegradable materials** are reshaping this industry.

- **Crucial Positions**: Recycling engineers (optimize recycling systems), waste reduction specialists (design systems for minimizing waste), sustainability consultants (help businesses manage waste and adopt greener practices).

37. Healthcare Technology

The integration of **artificial intelligence (AI), machine learning (ML),** and **wearable devices** is revolutionizing **healthcare technology**. Digital health tools and remote diagnostics are improving patient care while reducing costs.

- **Crucial Positions**: Health IT specialists (integrate tech solutions into healthcare systems), digital health app developers (build health-monitoring tools), AI diagnostics analysts (develop AI systems for disease detection).

38. 3D Printing

3D printing is disrupting manufacturing by enabling the on-demand production of parts, tools, and even prosthetics. 3D printing is being adopted in industries such as **aerospace, healthcare,** and **automotive**.

- **Crucial Positions**: 3D printing engineers (design printed products), product developers (customize manufacturing with 3D technology), additive manufacturing specialists (focus on using 3D printing for industrial applications).

39. Digital Payments

With the rise of **mobile payments**, **contactless transactions**, and **cryptocurrencies**, the digital payments industry is undergoing rapid growth. Companies and consumers are moving away from cash, creating demand for **secure, fast, and reliable payment systems**.

- **Crucial Positions**: Digital payments consultants (design and implement secure payment systems), payment platform developers (build digital payment infrastructures), FinTech strategists (analyze trends in financial technology).

40. Remote Work Services

The shift to **remote work** has created new opportunities for companies providing **virtual office solutions**, **digital collaboration tools**, and **remote management systems**. With distributed teams becoming the norm, the infrastructure for remote work has expanded rapidly.

- **Crucial Positions**: Remote work consultants (help companies transition to remote models), collaboration tool developers (build digital platforms for remote teams), digital office managers (oversee virtual office operations).

41. Influencer Marketing

Social media influencers are now integral to digital marketing strategies, offering brands direct access to specific target audiences. The rise of platforms like **Instagram**, **TikTok**, and **YouTube** has solidified influencer marketing as a major industry.

- **Crucial Positions**: Influencer marketing managers (manage partnerships between brands and influencers), social media strategists (design campaigns leveraging influencers), content monetization experts (help influencers generate revenue from their platforms).

42. Fashion Tech

The fashion industry is merging with technology to create **smart textiles**, **wearable tech**, and **sustainable fashion** practices. From **AI-powered design** to **virtual try-ons**, tech is redefining how fashion is created, sold, and worn.

- **Crucial Positions**: Fashion technologists (integrate tech into clothing), wearable tech developers (design smart garments with embedded sensors), sustainable fashion consultants (help brands reduce their environmental impact).

43. Smart Infrastructure

Smart infrastructure integrates IoT, data analytics, and AI to make cities, buildings, and public services more efficient. Smart roads, intelligent buildings, and real-time monitoring are central to developing **sustainable urban environments**.

- **Crucial Positions**: Smart infrastructure planners (integrate IoT into cities), IoT developers (build smart city technologies), urban data analysts (use data to optimize urban services).

44. Autonomous Drones

Autonomous drones are revolutionizing industries such as **logistics**, **agriculture**, **military**, and **entertainment** by offering unmanned, remote-operated solutions for delivery, monitoring, and surveillance.

- **Crucial Positions**: Drone operators (manage drone fleets), drone software developers (build systems for autonomous drones), logistics coordinators (integrate drones into delivery networks).

45. Clean Water Technology

Clean water technology addresses the global need for access to safe drinking water. Innovations in **desalination, water purification**, and **wastewater management** are creating jobs in environmental engineering.

- **Crucial Positions**: Water resource engineers (design systems for water purification), environmental scientists (work on water sustainability), desalination technicians (operate desalination plants).

46. Quantum Computing

Quantum computing is an emerging field with the potential to solve complex problems far beyond the capabilities of classical computers. Its applications in **cryptography**, **drug discovery**, and **logistics optimization** could revolutionize several industries.

- **Crucial Positions**: Quantum computer scientists (develop quantum algorithms), quantum hardware engineers (build quantum computing devices), cryptography experts (use quantum computing for secure communication).

47. 5G Technology

5G networks are expanding, offering faster, more reliable mobile connectivity that will enable advancements in everything from **IoT devices** to **smart cities**. The deployment of 5G infrastructure is driving massive job growth.

- **Crucial Positions**: 5G infrastructure engineers (design and deploy 5G networks), telecommunications technicians (maintain 5G hardware), IoT network developers (create devices that connect via 5G).

48. Legal Tech (continued)

Legal Tech is transforming the traditional legal landscape through automation, AI, and digital solutions for legal services. Innovations include **smart contracts**, **AI-driven legal research**, and **automated document analysis**, which are reducing costs and increasing efficiency in legal processes.

- **Crucial Positions**: **Legal technologists** (implement and manage legal technology tools), **Smart contract developers** (create self-executing contracts using blockchain), **AI legal analysts** (use AI to perform legal research), **E-discovery specialists** (manage digital evidence and document review using technology).

49. Bioinformatics

Bioinformatics combines biology, computer science, and information technology to analyze and interpret complex biological data, particularly in genomics, drug development, and personalized medicine. As healthcare becomes more data-driven, bioinformatics is essential in unlocking insights from DNA and other biological information.

- **Crucial Positions**: **Bioinformaticians** (develop algorithms to analyze biological data), **Genomics data analysts** (interpret genetic data for personalized medicine), **Biostatisticians** (use statistical techniques to analyze and model biological experiments), **Pharmaceutical bioinformatics experts** (help in drug discovery and optimization through computational biology).

50. Micro-Mobility

Micro-mobility refers to small, lightweight transportation solutions such as **e-scooters**, **bicycles**, and **e-bikes** designed for short-distance travel. As urban areas look to reduce traffic congestion and carbon emissions, micro-mobility solutions are becoming integral to smart city planning and public transportation systems.

- **Crucial Positions**: **Micro-mobility fleet managers** (oversee operations and maintenance of shared fleets), **Urban mobility planners** (integrate micro-mobility into transportation systems), **Micro-mobility engineers** (develop and improve electric scooters, e-bikes, and other personal transportation devices), **Sustainability consultants** (work with cities to implement eco-friendly transportation solutions).

The potential for creating new jobs in the next decade is substantial in each of these sectors, particularly because of technological advances. AI, for instance, is expected to create millions of opportunities in specialized areas. The same holds true in a number of other key sectors, like robotics, where about half a million new jobs are anticipated in the next decade, according to the World Economic Forum. Similarly, the renewable energy sector will need about 1.3 million new workers just in the demand-side energy efficiency part of the business (which is only a fraction of the sector) between now and 2030, according to a report by the US Department of Labor.

Universal Competencies:

1. Data Analysis and AI Integration: No matter the sector, the contemporary workforce will glean insights from data, with the decisions they make based on those insights impacting everything from human lives to industry bottom lines. As datasets grow in size and our capacity to process them using artificial intelligence matures, we will look to data scientists, machine learning specialists, and AI engineers to do the crucial work of converting the increased quantity and quality of available information into usable insights.

2. Eco-Friendliness: Climate change is profoundly remaking the world we live in. Pay no mind to apparent divides—between report readers like me and real-world interlocutors like you—that's one big thing that's happening. To mitigate the effects of that big thing in the real world, we need cross-sectional jobs across all industries focusing on the climate.

The upcoming employment landscape will increasingly be influenced by industries that leverage technology and concentrate on sustainable innovation. While several sectors—including AI, cloud computing, and biotechnology—are experiencing phenomenal growth, others like legal tech, smart cities, and micro-mobility will likely emerge as important engines of recruitment during the next decade. Therefore, whether you're a professional already in the workforce or a job seeker, it's vital not only to acquire technical skills but also to develop hybrid skills that combine technical expertise with creativity and critical thinking.

To get ready for the next huge installment of jobs, we will need not just a single set of a few job skills but a vast array of abilities. We will need skills that are adaptable and that can keep pace not only with our mind-bogglingly fast-changing workplaces but also with an often equally effective world of technological change happening in our homes and on our streets. We will need continuous learning and the ability to get through the technological, sustainable, and global collaborative morass that we all seem to be heading toward.

ACKNOWLEDGEMENT

In creating this book, I have been fortunate to draw upon the wisdom and expertise of an exceptional global network of partners and friends. Their contributions, both direct and indirect, have profoundly shaped this work, and I am deeply grateful for their influence. The following deserve special acknowledgements:

Kanth Krishnan, Managing Director at Accenture, whose visionary leadership and penetrating insights in technology services have been truly inspiring. His deep industry knowledge has substantially enriched this book's content.

Jeff Pappas, Managing Director at Newmark, who offered vital perspectives on the global real estate market landscape, bringing unmatched expertise to our exploration of diverse business environments.

Haitao Qi, Chairman of Devott Research and Advisory, whose illuminating insights on technology innovations and market trends, particularly in Asia, have been invaluable.

Charles Aird, former head of Outsourcing and Managed Services at PwC, whose comprehensive knowledge and strategic vision in outsourcing services have deeply informed my understanding of this crucial business function.

Mike Beares, Founder and Board Chairman of Clutch.co, whose entrepreneurial vision and commitment to connecting businesses with optimal service providers have significantly influenced my perspective on business connectivity.

Marc Schwarz, an industry pioneer in technology services, global sourcing, and innovation since the 1980s. His distinguished career spanning PwC, Deloitte, HP, and Sun Microsystems has yielded insights that have transformed our clients' businesses.

The merits of this book are a direct reflection of this exceptional global network, while any shortcomings are entirely my own responsibility.

Finally, I must express my deepest gratitude to my wife, Biyu, whose unwavering support and understanding have been fundamental to this endeavor. The intensive writing process, reminiscent of my doctoral dissertation at Yale twenty-five years ago, was made possible by her continuous encouragement. She remains the driving force behind both my professional growth and personal fulfillment.

ABOUT THE AUTHOR

Stephan S. Sunn

Stephan Sunn serves as Executive Partner at
Sanford Black Advisory, a leading global
business and investment consultancy. He advises
companies worldwide on growth strategy,
marketing and sales optimization, innovation
monetization, strategic partnerships, and mergers
& acquisitions. Co-founding Davidson Global &
Co. with partners from premier consulting firms
and technology companies, Stephan works to
make high-quality consulting services more
affordable and accessible to startups and SMEs
globally.

Over two decades, he has led 120+ corporate consulting engagements,
advised 48 cities and technology parks, and collaborated with 500+ service
providers. His portfolio spans 50+ international marketing projects, 20+
M&A transactions, and 40+ global events across technology services
sectors. Stephan holds a honorary leadership role at Devott Co., China's
foremost private research firm in IT and technology services, and serves as a
Director of the China IT and Outsourcing Association. His clients range from
Fortune 500 corporations to startups in both developed and emerging
markets.

A graduate of the University of Science and Technology of China (USTC)
with a Bachelor of Science degree, and Yale University with both Master of

Science and Ph.D., Stephan is a frequent speaker at global conferences and a prolific author in his professional fields.

BOOKS BY THIS AUTHOR

<u>Emerging Niche Industries</u>
<u>High-Growth Sectors Of The Future Jobs</u>

The book "Emerging Niche Industries – High-Growth Sectors of Future Jobs"
provides a roadmap for professionals seeking lucrative careers in
specialized industries poised for significant expansion. It begins by
highlighting the paradigm shift in career success, emphasizing adaptability,
continuous learning, and the alignment of passion with prosperity as crucial
to thriving in a dynamic job market. Traditional career paths are contrasted
with niche careers, which allow for rapid growth, cross-border
opportunities, and high earning potential in unique, underserved fields.
Key areas of exploration include emerging technologies, such as artificial
intelligence, cybersecurity, and biotechnology, which drive demand for
highly specialized roles. The book also delves into the creative economy,
where digital content creation and online education offer unprecedented
monetization avenues, and sustainability sectors like renewable energy, food
tech, and green building, which are critical in addressing global
environmental challenges.
Additionally, the text addresses the financial sector's evolution through
fintech, digital assets, and ESG investing, where professionals can shape
sustainable investment trends. Niche opportunities in luxury markets and
healthcare innovation also showcase high-reward roles for those with
specialized skills and global perspectives.
For aspiring professionals, the book advocates for interdisciplinary skills,
ethical considerations, and a global mindset as essential strategies for
excelling in niche industries that balance wealth creation with meaningful,
future-focused impact.

Asian Startup Failures:
Lessons And Case Studies For Success

The book "Failures of Asian Startups: Key Lessons and Case Studies" examines the reasons for startup failures across Asia, emphasizing challenges stemming from internal dynamics, the broader Asian business environment, and country-specific factors. The book categorizes common failures into several themes, such as strategic misalignment, financial mismanagement, leadership struggles, and market entry challenges.

One prominent theme is the difficulty startups face in scaling operations due to Asia's diverse regulatory landscapes and fragmented markets, where cultural nuances and regulatory differences often hinder consistent growth. Many startups fail by adopting Western business models without adequate localization, leading to poor customer adoption and operational setbacks. Additionally, excessive reliance on venture capital for rapid scaling often pressures startups into unsustainable growth practices, such as high customer acquisition costs without a focus on retention, undermining long-term viability.

Through detailed case studies, including companies like Honestbee, Zilingo, and Ofo, the book underscores the importance of local adaptability, sustainable unit economics, and resilient operational models. It advocates for strategies like in-depth market research, localization, and balancing growth with profitability to foster sustainable success. By learning from these common pitfalls, the next generation of Asian entrepreneurs can build more resilient and culturally attuned businesses for the complex and dynamic Asian markets.

Competing For The Growth:
How Cities And Technology Parks Attract Global Trades And Investments

This book serves as a guidebook for city planners, economic development professionals, tech park builders, and public officials who aim to create thriving innovation communities that attract global trade and stimulate investments. It offers a structured path that begins with intangible factors like vision setting and partnership alignment and extends to pilots and full-blown magnet programs.

The book provides real-life instructions to help put these ideas into practice, including effective strategies for attracting rapidly growing businesses and talent, creating a setting that promotes innovation and entrepreneurship, fostering a competitive and appealing business climate, and building a globally recognized brand and reputation.

The author emphasizes that cities and tech parks must play to their strengths and assets to compete and win in the global arena. The race for relevance is on, and the window of opportunity to determine the outcome is closing. Cities and companies have what they need to succeed, and with the options, relationships, and guidance provided in this book, city managers and tech park authorities can make the decisions necessary to lead their communities to success in the world investment and trade arena.

Searching The New Profits: How The US SMEs And Startups Succeed In The Emerging Markets

In the face of global market turbulence and domestic uncertainties, American small and medium-sized businesses (SMBs) and startups have significant growth opportunities in emerging markets. However, these markets also present unique challenges. This handbook provides a semi-analytical and semi-prescriptive approach to help American SMBs and entrepreneurs succeed in these rapidly expanding markets. Conversely, governments, technology parks, and corporations in emerging countries can utilize this book to learn how to collaborate with U.S. companies in their markets to serve their customers effectively.

The book covers essential themes such as researching and identifying matching markets, choosing the appropriate market entry mode, local marketing and sales tactics, effective risk management, establishing an active and reputable presence in the local market, ensuring full legal compliance, avoiding political involvement, talent search and retention, and balancing standardization and localization. The final chapter shares valuable lessons from decades of business practices, acknowledging that readers may have different perspectives on these topics. Expanding knowledge through diverse viewpoints is beneficial for U.S. SMB and startup leaders. Despite the challenges, penetrating foreign markets can be highly profitable, and U.S. enterprises have a reasonable chance of success by capitalizing on the vast potential of these rapidly growing territories.

Cracking The Winning Codes: How Global Vendors Win In The US Digital And Outsourcing Markets

This book serves as a comprehensive guide for international technology and outsourcing companies seeking to enter and succeed in the highly competitive U.S. market. It emphasizes the importance of adapting to the unique American business culture, which values innovation, diversity, relationships, customer-centricity, and results-oriented management. The guide highlights the need to navigate the complex U.S. regulatory landscape, including federal and state laws, as well as key legislations such as FCPA, SOX, and HIPAA.

The book covers essential topics such as understanding American business culture, complying with legal requirements, developing effective marketing strategies, employing successful sales techniques, addressing cultural differences, and managing risks associated with entering a new market. Additionally, it encourages the use of innovative tactics to differentiate from competitors and gain market share.

A special section titled "The Lessons" shares the author's personal experiences and insights, providing practical execution tips that focus on solution-oriented approaches, leveraging referrals and testimonials, managing communication costs, delivering higher quality than promised, and investing in proven local sales leaders.

By adhering to the core principles of understanding buyer preferences, continuous innovation, human capital development, risk management, customer-centricity, and resilient operations, global providers can successfully navigate and thrive in the lucrative U.S. market

Win More Deals In The Digital Era: How Martech And Salestech Improve Marketing And Sales

In the new economy, businesses must navigate the complex landscape of Marketing Technology (Martech) and Sales Technology (Salestech) to stay competitive and drive growth. "Win More Deals in Digital Age" provides a comprehensive guide for leveraging these technologies to enhance customer experiences, streamline processes, and boost revenue across international markets.

The book explores the convergence of marketing, sales, and technology, emphasizing the importance of data-driven decision-making and cross-functional collaboration. It offers strategies for overcoming challenges in digital transformation, such as resistance to change and skills gaps, while also addressing the unique considerations of global expansion and localization. The authors predict future trends in Martech and Salestech, including the increasing role of AI, personalization, and emerging technologies like AR/VR and voice interfaces. Through real-world success stories from global brands like Coca-Cola, Sephora, and Airbnb, readers gain valuable insights into harnessing the power of these technologies for business success. This book serves as an essential resource for executives and professionals seeking to navigate the digital ecosystem and drive growth in the international marketplace.

Renovations Or Revolutions: Impacts Of Latest AI On BPO And Contact Centers

The book "Renovation or Revolution? Impacts of Latest AI on BPO and Contact-centers Industries" provides an in-depth exploration of the transformative potential of artificial intelligence (AI) within the business process outsourcing (BPO) and contact center industries. It emphasizes the importance of early adoption, customization, and localization of AI solutions to gain a competitive edge in the global marketplace. The book highlights the evolving role of human agents, who will focus on complex problem-solving and relationship-building, while AI handles routine tasks. It also discusses the development of AI expertise within organizations and the ethical considerations surrounding AI implementation.

The authors present a roadmap for incorporating AI, underlining the need for a clear vision, employee training, and continuous improvement. Looking ahead, the book envisions a future of collaborative human-AI partnerships, hyper-personalization, and proactive customer engagement. It stresses that embracing AI is crucial for BPO and contact center companies to achieve sustainable growth and remain competitive in the international arena. The book serves as a comprehensive guide for executives navigating the AI revolution in the global business services industry.

Risky Reefs In The Ocean Of Global Markets: Common Mistakes Emerging Markets' Companies In Their Global Expansions

This book provides a comprehensive roadmap for emerging market companies venturing into global expansion. It highlights common pitfalls across strategic planning, finance, operations, human resources, marketing, technology, legal/ethics, and risk management. The book emphasizes thorough market research, cultural adaptation, local partnerships, brand building, innovation investment, and long-term vision.
As the global landscape evolves, it anticipates trends like digitization, sustainability integration, and talent acquisition challenges. The book provides corporate decision-makers with insights and best practices to navigate complexities, mitigate risks, and foster sustainable growth while driving innovation and progress internationally.

The AI Revolution In B2B Marketing And Sales: Disruptions Of AI In The Conventional B2B Markets

This professional guidance provides a comprehensive playbook for leveraging artificial intelligence (AI) to drive measurable results in B2B marketing and sales strategies. With insights from real-world case studies spanning diverse industries and business sizes, it explores AI's transformative impact on understanding the AI-empowered buyer, delivering personalized omnichannel experiences, boosting sales productivity, and optimizing operations.

The book offers a strategic framework for successful AI implementation, covering data readiness, talent acquisition, governance, and ethical considerations. Globally applicable principles foster human-AI collaboration, enabling organizations worldwide to harness AI's potential ethically and profitably in the B2B domain.

Promotor, Suppressor Or Neutralizer Impact Of Latest AI And Geopolitics On Global Outsourcing

This book explores how artificial intelligence (AI) and geopolitics are transforming the global outsourcing industry. It analyzes the strategic implications of AI for outsourcing operations, delivery models, talent management, and client relationships. The impact of geopolitical forces like trade tensions, political instability, and regulatory shifts on risk mitigation and geographic diversification is examined.

Emerging business models combining AI and human expertise, niche services, innovation through collaboration, workforce upskilling, and ethical AI governance are highlighted. The book provides a strategic roadmap for international outsourcing providers to navigate challenges, seize opportunities, and drive sustainable growth in this era of technological disruption and evolving geopolitical dynamics.

Pricing For Profitability And Growth: Mastering Pricing Strategies In Technology And Services Globally

This book explores how companies in the technology and service sectors can leverage strategic pricing to drive growth and profitability. It advocates moving beyond traditional cost-plus pricing to adopt value-based approaches that align pricing with customer perceptions of value. Key recommendations include: conducting thorough market research to understand customer needs and willingness to pay; segmenting customers and offering differentiated pricing tiers; leveraging data and analytics for dynamic pricing optimization; and aligning sales, marketing and pricing teams around a cohesive value proposition. The book emphasizes the importance of quantifying and communicating value to justify premium pricing.

Looking to the future, the book highlights how artificial intelligence and machine learning will transform pricing capabilities, enabling more personalized and responsive pricing strategies. It cautions against common pitfalls like failing to account for competitive responses or neglecting the psychology of pricing. Ultimately, the authors argue that pricing is a critical strategic capability that requires ongoing experimentation, cross-functional collaboration, and a willingness to adapt to changing market conditions. By taking a customer-centric, data-driven approach to pricing, technology and service companies can gain a powerful lever for sustainable growth and competitive advantage.

GovTech, Governance Technology: Unlocking Competitive Advantage For Cities And Tech Parks

This book dives into GovTech's potential to revolutionize government and urban development. By leveraging data, AI, and e-government platforms, GovTech can streamline processes, boost transparency, and even enhance citizen engagement. The book emphasizes collaboration between government, businesses, academia, and citizens to create a thriving GovTech ecosystem. Success stories from Estonia and Singapore showcase how GovTech can attract investment, streamline business operations, and fuel economic growth. Furthermore, the book explores GovTech's role in fostering innovation hubs and simplifying business registrations, particularly for SMEs. It also delves into the power of data-driven governance and AI to transform public services and policymaking. Finally, the human aspect is crucial. Building a skilled workforce, managing cultural shifts, and promoting digital literacy are all emphasized for GovTech to reach its full potential.